PICTURE PALACE

PICTURE PALACE

A Social History of the Cinema

AUDREY FIELD

gb

GENTRY BOOKS · LONDON

First published 1974
© Audrey Field 1974
ISBN 0 85614 029 5
All rights reserved. Without written permission
from Gentry Books Ltd., this volume, or any part
of it, may not be reproduced by any means
or in any form.

Published by Gentry Books Limited
15 Tooks Court, London EC4A 1LA
Designed by Brian Roll
Printed by
Cox & Wyman Ltd, London, Fakenham and Reading

To
Minnie F. McIntosh

Acknowledgements

I am grateful to nearly all my friends and relations for their advice and encouragement in the pleasurable task of writing this book.

In the world of the cinema, besides those who are mentioned in the book, I would like to thank Mr R. H. Dewes, lately Trade Relations Adviser to Rank Leisure Services Limited, Mr David Samuelson, FBKS, BSc, Chairman of the Incorporated Association of Kinematograph Manufacturers, and the Secretary and staff of the British Board of Film Censors, my kind former colleagues.

I must also add a special tribute to the late lamented *Kinematograph Weekly*, known affectionately to the trade, and hereinafter, as *Kine Weekly* or *The Kine*, which gobbled up *Lantern Weekly* in the early years of the century and has now in its turn been absorbed by *CINEMATV Today*.

Contents

Introduction

**1
In the
Beginning**
page 11

**2
In Time
of War**
page 43

**3
The Restless
Twenties**
page 71

**4
The Anxious
Thirties**
page 103

**5
Chaos
comes again**
page 131

Bibliography

Index

Illustrations

	opposite page
Projectionist's certificate of proficiency, 1912	32
A patron counts the cost—cartoon from the *Kine Weekly*, 1922 (*by courtesy of CINEMATV Today*)	33
'Throwaways and Striking Novelties' from *How to Run a Picture Theatre* (*by courtesy of CINEMATV Today*)	48
'A Few Typical Fronts' from *How to Run a Picture Theatre* (*by courtesy of CINEMATV Today*)	49
The proprietor of a family picture house, with his family and staff, 1924 (*Kidd, Photographer, Aberdeen*)	80
A town picture house, 1926 (*White, Holme & Co., Dundee*)	81
The projection room of the Tower Annexe, Peckham, *circa* 1923 (*Robert Pulman, FBKS*)	81
Queueing for *Trader Horn* outside the Empire, Leicester Square, 1931 (*MGM-EMI Distributors Ltd*)	96
The interior of the Empire, Leicester Square, 1928-60 (*MGM-EMI Distributors Ltd.*)	96
Charlie Chaplin draws the crowds at the Glasgow Coliseum, 1931 (*George Outram & Co. Ltd*)	97
Queueing in the rain for *The Great Ziegfeld*, 1936 (*George Outram & Co. Ltd*)	128
A projectionist at work—Bert Mayell at the Abbey Cinema, Netley, Hants, 1940 (*by courtesy of Bert Mayell*)	129
The projection-room staff of the Gaumont, Chadwell Heath, 1943 (*Robert Pulman, FBKS*)	129
Children queueing for a Kinema Club Matinée, 1948 (*by courtesy of CINEMATV Today*)	144
Queues at Giffnock, when the suburban cinemas re-opened in September, 1939 (*George Outram & Co. Ltd*)	144
Carlisle House—home of the British Board of Film Censors, 1936-41 (*British Board of Film Censors*)	145

Introduction

The cinema is not what it was. Everyone who is old enough to have memories of cinema-going knows that. It is better than it was, because it has discarded superficial sentimentality in favour of brutal frankness and looking life squarely in the face. It is worse than it was, because unrestrained sex and violence are its stock-in-trade. It all depends upon your point of view—which, in turn, depends largely upon your age.

But in any case, you are talking about films. You are not talking about the cinematograph theatre itself, for you only go there to see a film which you have reason to believe will please or interest you; and when you do go you take your surroundings very much for granted, unless they fall short of the standard of comfort and efficiency you have been led to expect. It was not always so. The cinema, indeed, is not what it was. But what *was* it? If you are very young, you do not know. But if you are middle-aged or older you can remember with pleasure that focus of social life which had a warmth, a vividness, a glamour, over and above the mixed bag of good, bad and indifferent films that were shown in it.

This book is not primarily about films. Rather, it is an affectionate look back at some aspects of cinemas, their angry critics, their anxious guardians, their dedicated audiences and the resourceful and hard-working people who ran them, to the benefit of almost every man, woman and child in the country, in the days when, in the world of popular entertainment, there was no rival to the movie show.

1
In the Beginning

The era of short films such as *The Great Train Robbery* and *Rescued by Rover*. Meliès filmed the Coronation of Edward VII in 1902. The first *Ben Hur* was made in America in 1908. 1909 saw the début of Mary Pickford as a child star. Tom Mix appeared in 1910, Charlie Chaplin in 1913 and Douglas Fairbanks and Rudolph Valentino a year later. The first *Quo Vadis* appeared in Italy in 1912: it presaged the end of the short feature, for it ran for two hours.

1
In the Beginning

In the earliest years of the century, Top People seem to have been slow to notice that the film fever which was already endemic in France and the United States had taken a hold upon this country too. In 1896 *The Times* had introduced the new discovery, concurrently with the picture show which was drawing big audiences at the Regent Street Polytechnic:

> The Cinematograph, which is the invention of MM. A. and L. Lumière, is a contrivance belonging to the same family as Edison's Kinetoscope and the old 'Wheel of Life', but in a rather higher stage of development. The spectator no longer gazes through a narrow aperture at the changing picture, but has it presented to him full size on a large screen. The principle, however, is much the same, consisting simply of passing rapidly before the eye a series of pictures representing the successive stages of the action of the changing scene that has to be reproduced.

After pointing out that one good thing to reproduce is a crowd of people moving along the street, it goes on,

Another subject that lends itself very effectively to this treatment is a railway train entering and stopping at a station. The movements of the people leaving the carriage and the bustle on the platform are reproduced with lifelike fidelity.

Put like that, it does not sound a very exhilarating entertainment, hardly the sort of thing to create a panic, as it did when a picture of a train coming out of a station was shown to an audience in Paris; or even to make a small boy burst into tears of fright and be taken home instantly, as happened to my friend John when, a few years later, he was taken as a great treat to see this very scene, the high spot of an entertainment at the Watford music-hall.

The Times relapsed into silence for another eight years. After all, why should it concern itself with a childish novelty that was not expected to last (the Lumière brothers themselves believed that it would not last) and that in the meantime appealed most of all to 'persons who appeared to belong to the labouring classes', for so the grander sort of journalists were apt to express themselves in those days.

The next glimpse of cinematograph history which *The Times* offers us is an unhappy letter from Mr W. Friese Greene on 6 April 1904, complaining that the new edition of the *Encyclopaedia Britannica* had not done him justice. He had been working on this invention for over twenty years, took out his first patent in 1889, for a camera for taking pictures on celluloid, and in 1893 took out a further patent. 'Such patent not only covered the apparatus for taking the pictures, but also the apparatus for the projecting of the same upon a screen. This, in connection with my patent of 1889, is the master patent on the cinematograph.'

In spite of all his hard work, the unfortunate Mr Friese Greene died penniless. Inventors had been working away independently in Europe and America, often with no idea of competing in a race. It is still a matter for debate who actually won. What is certain is that in this country the ensuing race to exploit the commercial projection of motion pictures was won by Edison. This fact, together with the formidable obstacles to film production in Europe during the First World War, ultimately ensured the supremacy of American motion pictures for many years to come.

However, this was still in the future. What the letter does make clear is that the fascinating world of motion pictures was now

In the Beginning

well advanced. An article in the *Encyclopaedia Britannica* does suggest something not beneath 'the Establishment's' notice after all. Sure enough, only two years later, in June 1906, *The Times* was invited to a very unusual Press show, and it went.

> On Saturday [it reports in the issue of 6 June], a few representatives of the Press were invited by Mr Charles Urban to see at his office in Rupert Street an exhibition on the bioscope of certain photographs which, for various reasons, are not suitable for public entertainments. The series showing the bull fights at Madrid attended by the King and Queen of Spain made it clear that what the public sees at the Alhambra is only a small part of the whole, from which many sensational details have been wisely omitted. Which series, the complete or the expurgated, gives the better idea of a bull fight there can be no question, as there can be no question that Mr Urban did right in omitting many of the scenes from which the camera was unable to emulate Queen Victoria and turn away its eyes...

We are looking into an unfamiliar country—our own country, in our own century, and yet as remote from us today as the planet Mars.

A year later, 'the pictures' came to the newspaper men, when the Kearton brothers gave a special show of their films of birds at the Institute of Journalists. The audience proved to be less than hard-boiled, for they 'could not forbear a cheer when the sedge-warbler, finding his mate on the nest, passed on the food, which she in turn passed on to the young'.

The 'cinematograph views' in general were not so well worth a cheer, but less sophisticated audiences cheered them all the same. As long as the picture moved, it hardly mattered what it was—omnibuses in the street, trains in the station, very primitive short comedies and trick films and, little by little, the first real stories. Cecil Hepworth's *Rescued by Rover*, made in 1904 at a cost of £7.13.9, has attained a place in all histories of film. The Thunderer ignored it, but it did take notice a few years later of one of the other 'manufacturers' who had hastened to follow the fashion of making films about heroic and resourceful animals, for this venture came to a bad end and finished up in the Coroner's court where solid news is recorded. In the issue of 23 April 1907 we learn that the Clarendon Film Company had borrowed a railway engine from the station master at Stoat's Nest on the London, Brighton and South Coast Railway (without the knowledge of the railway company) to film the story of a dog which set the signals at danger to save its master who was lying injured on the line. A Mr William Zeitz was playing the part of the injured man. The driver said afterwards that no one had told him that there really was a man on the line. The train did not stop in time and Mr Zeitz was killed. An almost incredible story of the restrictive days before the railways belonged to the people.

The uneventful, unnoticed short films were by now being shown anywhere that would give them house-room, in village halls, in church halls, as part of the variety programme in music-halls, in schools, in empty shops with the front windows knocked out and replaced by porticos, in tents, and by travelling showmen in magnificent portable theatres specially designed for the purpose. The largest of these held about 800 people, and they and their successors went on touring the country in summer and settling down on permanent sites in winter till the end of the First World War. In considering the nature of the world of the movies as it has evolved through the years, it never does to forget the travelling showmen, many of whom did not consider themselves as purveyors of high art, but rather of signs and portents, of two-headed monsters and bearded ladies and other phenomena outside the common run of nature. In the more excitable sort of trailer we can still hear the voice of the fairground barker, 'Walk up! Walk up! Never before on any screen! The film they said could never be made! Salacious! Shocking! Stupendous!'

One way or another, it does seem that everyone who wanted to 'go to the pictures' now had a chance of doing so. A surprising number did want to, and the first specially erected permanent buildings arrived. There is considerable difference of opinion about which was the very first of these places. Cecil Hepworth, talking to the National Council for Public Morals in 1917, only about ten years after the event, said that it was Terry's, near the old Tivoli in the Strand, but in those days it was quite possible for one corner of this small country not to know what another corner was doing, so some other building, somewhere, may well have escaped his notice.

The new pictures houses were a particular source of joy to the 'persons who appeared to belong to the labouring classes'. In the field of organized entertainment, they had never in all their lives had such a delightful time. Not that they had not had any fun before: they had. We know—for many of them are still alive to prove it—that they were a dogged and resilient breed, adept at making the most of what they had. Many of the grown-ups went quite often to the music-halls, of which there was at least one in any sizeable town; the children went to the Girls' Brigade, the Boys' Brigade, the Sunday School outings, the indifferent amateur shows organized by the churches, and they might be taken by their fathers on Sunday morning to hear the band in the park. And above all, most of the fathers went to the pub. They could go pretty well when they liked, slipping in for a quick tot of gin on the way to work, or lingering on till midnight after work. In the poor parts of English cities many of the wives went too, and the little children. A friend of mine who was a child in Peckham at the turn of the century tells me that her mother, 'carrying' and with a small child at foot, used to accompany her father, taking with her the potatoes for peeling and the peas for shelling for the family meal.

But we must not forget that life was very hard. It is no wonder that, on an average, the working man spent as much on drink as he did on rent. We know that housing was appallingly squalid and overcrowded, that consumption, as it was then called, was a scourge, that wages were minute and working hours long enough to make the present generation curl up and die. People did not get enough sleep because, after the day's work, there was not time for sleep *and* relaxation. Large numbers of the children ran wild in the street because there was no room for them in the home. They came home when they thought they would and went to bed when they liked. Or so it was among the poorest of the urban poor. Country life was no more affluent, but it did escape some of the worst evils of the dark and dirty slums.

Suddenly into all this came the delights of the 'penny gaff', the mesmeric fascination of the moving images on the shiny screen in the dark place. The dark place may not have been very like a palace: one cannot expect a stately pleasure dome to rise like magic out of a city slum. The seats were hard, the air soon became smoky and foul, the company inside was as rough and noisy as the company outside, which meant that an intruder from more opulent districts would have found it uncongenial. And indeed, even among the local inhabitants in those early days it was not considered the place for a respectable young girl on her own, and anyone who did not want his pocket picked had to take care. My friend Bette of Peckham Rye, as a young lass, was advised not to go to the penny gaff by herself, so of course she went, but only once.

But for all its shortcomings, it was like Aladdin's cave, or the crock of gold at the end of the rainbow. And for a penny or less it was the cheapest evening's entertainment that could now be obtained. For one could not spin out half a pint of beer to last a whole evening, and gin, on which one's grandfather could have got 'drunk for a penny, dead drunk for twopence', now cost threepence a tot; so sometimes father deserted the pub to bear his family company. It was cheap enough for the children on their own, with their own pocket-money: a halfpenny sometimes, or sometimes no money changed hands at all, the price of admission being a clean empty bottle or jam jar. Even after the First World War they could get in here and there for a bottle instead of cash.

For the children, the whole thing was the most glorious adventure. The commonest alternative amusement had been running about the streets in excited, noisy, high-spirited games, which was splendid in summer, with street traffic as easy to avoid as it was then, but in dark winter days had its drawbacks even for the unquenchable high spirits of childhood. Fidgeting and dancing up and down in the queue in excited anticipation was better, even if it was rather colder; and when they got inside, warm and dry, and the entertainment began, it was like having Christmas at least every Saturday of the year. It was not particularly safe, in the roughest and most primitive houses of all, when the door opened and they went storming in yelling; but life is a perilous business at the best of times, and it was doubly so then. As Mr Newbould of the Cinematograph Exhibitors' Association remarked about ten years later, one had to consider, in assessing the merits and demerits of cinema-going, what people would have been doing instead, and the hazards of the streets by night, with their thieves and hooligans and prostitutes, and the stalls of the street traders an open invitation to pilfering, were far more instant and real.

There was, however, one danger imminent in the picture shows

In the Beginning

of those days, wherever they took place, and not in the open air—the hazard of fire. The very thought of nitrate film stock going up in a burst of flame is quite terrifying. Most ordinary members of the audience did not think about it till it happened, but we have newspaper reports of the effect when it did. Said *The Times* on 15 June 1909:

> ... A fire occurred last night at a cinematograph entertainment on premises in East India Dock-road occupied by the British Bioscope Company. As the operator was placing the first spool of film on the machine at the beginning of performance, the film came into contact with the hot chimney and at once flared up. There was immediately some excitement among the audience, but the people were conducted out of the building, leaving quietly and without panic. The operator succeeded in putting out the flames.

In London, in those early years, no cinema patron lost his life in a fire. But in an incident in Southsea two months later the outcome was tragic:

> A panic in which one child was killed and eight others were injured, took place on Saturday afternoon at the Victoria Hall, Southsea, during an exhibition of cinematograph views. Soon after the display began an electric wire 'fired' and caused the film to ignite. There was no real danger, for the operator extinguished the flames in a few minutes with a blanket and a bucket of water; but alarm was excited among the spectators, and some time passed before the efforts of the attendants and of the band, which continued to play with a view to reassure those present, induced many of those who were on the ground floor of the hall to return to their places. In the gallery were some 200 children, who rushed to the doors to make their escape. During the pressure a wooden partition gave way and a number of the children fell into a corridor. This incident increased the terror of the children, and they ran down a staircase and became wedged in a doorway at the bottom leading into the street...

It turned out at the inquest that the children were 'wedged' in the door because it was in fact locked. On this occasion, the locked door was no doubt an oversight, because all the special regulations which already existed to control entertainments where large numbers of children were present had been faithfully observed. But in the small converted shops it was not unknown for an exhibitor to try to run the whole show by himself, taking the money at the door, and then projecting the pictures, having locked the door to make sure nobody got in without paying. And it followed that accidents like the one at Southsea were not uncommon. The showmen did not want to kill or injure anybody, least of all themselves, and when the worst came to the worst they were resourceful and resolute in applying blankets and buckets of water—or even more sophisticated devices, such as the one demonstrated at the Hippodrome in 1908, in which a piece of cotton thread controlled a valve operating a water-sprinkler, and if a fire started the thread burned through and the valve opened. But these were, to put it mildly, unsatisfactory means of dealing with fires in which electric wires were usually involved. And most of the showmen were still inexperienced in handling nitrate stock and treated it as casually as if it had been the lantern slides of their youth. It was quite usual, for instance, to let the coils of film fall loose into a basket after they had been projected, and that in tents, as well as in permanent buildings.

It is obvious from the foregoing examples of accidents that panic rather than fire itself was the real danger. And in the worst loss of life in British cinema history till the end of the twenties—the crushing to death of sixteen children in a cinema in Barnsley in January 1908—there had been no fire and no panic, only a failure in the control of a crowd. The gallery became overcrowded with children and those at the top of the stairs were told to go down before those at the bottom had been cleared out of the way and shown to other seats.

The ordinary members of the audience probably never heard of any but the worst disasters, unless they happened in their own districts or involved their own family or friends. There is something to be said for slow, inadequate, and often only local, instead of national, media of communication: ignorance enabled many of them to enjoy going to the pictures without worrying too much about the possible consequences. And those who did envisage the worst took their courage in their hands and went all the same, though the trade was afraid that their fortitude might not last. But the local licensing authorities, notable worriers at the best of times, were properly alarmed and had long thought that 'there ought to be a law about it', more especially as for the past two or three years 'the pictures' had been bursting out of the schools and music-halls and fairground booths into new buildings erected for them. It was important that the actual buildings, as well as the projection booths, should be safe from the outset.

In fact, most of them were safe. Supremacy in the actual projection of motion pictures had put the American distributors in a very strong position to obtain preferential treatment for their films: most of what was shown in British picture-houses from 1908 onwards came from America. In consequence, the money available for the showmen's new empire was spent, not so much on manufacturing films, as they called it then, as in erecting good buildings in which to show them. This, in an old-established country full of homes less good than they ought to have been, was an important factor in ensuring the popularity of cinema-going when the first novelty of films had worn off. Succeeding decades did not think the early picture-houses good: they thought that the first had been too slavish imitations of theatres, and their successors too much like mere functional sheds for the projection of films. But one cannot hope to please immediate posterity, and by the standards of their own day most of them were well enough. According to *Kine Weekly*, and according to statistics, which cannot easily lie about matters of hard fact like loss of life, they were a great deal safer, on average, than the buildings used for the projection of films in the United States of America.

However, with the movie craze growing daily, it was inevitable that a few greedy, get-rich-quick operators should be cashing in on it, especially in districts where the other buildings were so bad that the patrons were not fussy. The London and Middlesex County Councils, specially alert about safety, and using all the powers available to them under existing legislation, had nevertheless been plagued with this problem and had been importuning the Home Secretary for a couple of years. At the beginning of 1909 the Theatres and Music Halls Committee of the London County Council was thinking of returning to the attack. The Buildings Committee considered that films were too lethal to be meddled with at all: it recommended inserting a clause in the regulations for the letting of schools that the schools were not available for cinematograph shows. They did not have second thoughts about the danger till they perceived that films could be educational and were not always 'mere entertainment'.

By now, however, the Cinematograph Act, 1909, was grinding its slow way into the statute book. The Home Office safety regulations made in pursuance of the Act were published in December and came into force at the beginning of the following year. From the beginning of 1910 the inflammable film in action was as closely confined as any slave of the lamp. It had to pass from one metal container to another, imprisoned in a fireproof cell, the projection room, known familiarly to the stewards of the mysteries as 'the box', or 'the bio-box', according to whether it was part of a cinema or had been added to a theatre or a music-hall for the filmed items in the programme. These dedicated men, the projectionists, had to have alternative ways of escape from the burning fiery furnace in case the worst came to the worst. It continued to be unwise to take liberties with nitrate film stock, which remained the medium for commercial cinematograph shows until about forty years later.

The new regulations made little difference to the London County Council, for they had maintained this sort of strict control over physical safety for some time, but many local authorities had been less scrupulous, and now all had to toe the line. It was high time, for the new picture palaces were springing up in all cities and sizeable towns. Edinburgh got its first in 1910, rather later than many of the great cities, and in the same year there was opened in London perhaps the most ambitiously luxurious palace to date. *The Times* was represented at the opening, and reported on 15 July 1910:

> Cinema House, the latest addition to the numerous cinematograph theatres which have sprung up in and around London, was opened yesterday afternoon by the Duchess of Portland, and many influential people were invited to the private view. The hall is in Oxford-street, almost opposite Peter Robinson's and within a minute's walk of the tube railways. It is well ventilated, and is panelled in oak, which, together with the delicate shade of 'Rose du Barri' velvet with which the seats are upholstered, gives a very restful and pleasing effect.

In the Beginning 23

There is a restaurant where light refreshments may be obtained at popular prices. The pictures shown yesterday were quite of the best, and as varied as they were interesting. A good deal of amusement was caused towards the end of the entertainment, for, quite unexpectedly, pictures of the opening ceremony were produced, and the majority of the audience had the unusual experience of witnessing their own arrival and subsequent deportment. These pictures were exhibited on the screen within 70 minutes after the photographs had been taken, and they were particularly clear.

A continuous performance will be given daily from 12 noon to 11 p.m. and the programme will be changed twice a week. Excellent seats can be obtained from 6d. to 2s.

Expensive for a cinema show in those days, but wonderful value, all the same, compared with any other kind of entertainment. And it is interesting to note that though the way of presenting the marvels of the screen changes from generation to generation, the marvels themselves do not change very much: about forty-five years later the audiences at Royal Command film performances were well pleased to see their fellow guests and their deportment on the screen via closed-circuit television.

The Times had had a busy day. Mr Charles Urban had now moved out of the 'office' where he used to give his Press shows into grander headquarters called Urbanora House, described in his trade advertisement as 'New and Sumptuous Premises . . . The most Complete, Replete and Up-to-Date Kinematograph Establishment in the World'; and at the invitation of Lord and Lady Grey, he had given to *The Times* and others 'a fine series of cinematograph pictures of Colonial life' to be used to encourage emigration to Canada.

It is all a long, long way from Shoreditch and the East India Dock Road and the little boys yelling and shouting 'Bang! Bang!' in the Westerns, and the bigger boys roaring approval or stamping impatience or, greatly daring, trying conclusions with the chucker-out. One has to recognize that already the cinema does its best to be all things to all men, women and children.

The Times Engineering Supplement was, on the whole, so well pleased with the cinematograph scene that, for the first time in its history, its devoted a whole article to the subject on 16 November

1910. It announced that the London County Council had just been called upon to grant eighty-seven new electric theatre licences 'and already some 5,000 of these displays are in operation in different parts of the kingdom'. The displays did not yet consist of feature films as we know them, for 'A good film may run to a length of 1,000 feet', and that, now eleven minutes of projection time, was even in those days only about a quarter of an hour.

The writer adds primly:

> It is important to bear in mind that, though this form of entertainment is still in its infancy, the cinematograph is not a mere means of amusement and recreation, but that it is destined to become a most valuable vehicle of instruction and that it will furnish a powerful educational medium in the hands of the teacher and the public lecturer.

This is ominous. But for the moment 'mere amusement and recreation' are still to the fore. So, now that so much has been done to ensure safety and comfort, is everybody happy, and can the fun go on? Not a bit of it. Only the audiences are happy. The local licensing authorities are still worrying, and now they are driving the cinema exhibitors nearly frantic, because they are in a much stronger position to do something about their various worries. For, besides requiring them to implement the safety regulations made by the Home Office from time to time, the Cinematograph Act of 1909 empowered them to attach any additional conditions to cinema licences that they thought fit—as long as the conditions were reasonable, and only a court of law could decide that they were not. True, the Home Office had drafted model conditions, but who was the Home Office to tell Glasgow and Liverpool and Manchester what they should or should not do?

The Home Office never said, for example, that there ought to be a fireman of the local authority's own fire service on the premises whenever the public were present, but the condition was widely imposed. It was as vexatious to the fireman to hang about with nothing to do as it was for the manager to have him there. This, at any rate, was the experience of a pioneer of the picture houses, who opened one in Dundee in 1912 partly because he loved films, but even more because he loved his fellow townsmen and hoped to give them an enjoyable alternative to getting drunk, a popular pastime which he deplored. He did not even know, on the opening night, that he had to have a licence, so next morning he and his partner were up before the court. They were pardoned and granted a licence. The enterprise prospered and drunkenness decreased—but not for the fireman on the spot, who had to drown his boredom: after all, however good the film, one does not want to see it every night. The resourceful exhibitor persuaded the Council to abandon this particular condition.

And also, now that physical safety was taken care of, there was more time to turn to the darling preoccupation of the British, moral safety, and in this respect we do not seem to have changed much: we worry about different aspects of the matter and are less certain than we were that we know the difference between right and wrong, but the acrimonious debate goes on with redoubled vigour.

From the moral point of view, the cinema was a fascinating focus of attention. For one thing, people were enjoying themselves in a dark place, and this was very fishy: how could you love darkness rather than light unless your deeds were evil? It is easy to dismiss this as merely morbid and prurient-minded; but if we have had experience of power cuts we realize that it makes better sense when light is hard come by and correspondingly cherished, as it was in 1912. And even in the music-halls, which could be better lit than the picture houses, there had been a running battle to prevent prostitutes and drunks from spoiling the show. The authorities did not like to contemplate the equivalent of a dark music-hall, especially with large numbers of children present to take an interest in what was going on. They wanted more light than seemed reasonable to people who understood the projection of motion pictures. If they could not get that, at least they could make the cinema as unlike a music-hall as possible, and with that end in view they were apt to restrict the music licence to instrumental music only (they had to concede that much, as the silent film was unthinkable without a pianist or an orchestra). This was vexatious to the exhibitors, for the link between 'the pictures' and variety was still very close, and also they liked to be able to accommodate the Christmas pantomime. The whole history of entertainment indicates that large buildings must be versatile—ready to accommodate *Messiah* and Harry Lauder, *Quo Vadis* and bingo and roller-skating and bowling and the Mozart Players and *Carry on Henry* and the parish operatic society and the Royal Shakespeare Company on tour.

What the local authorities did not always realize was that the person with the greatest interest in not letting the cinema become a disorderly house was the cinema proprietor himself. He did not like it any more than the publican likes it, and for the same reason: it would injure his reputation and probably put the cinema's licence in jeopardy and certainly lose the majority of the customers who did not want to get drunk or be pestered by prostitutes or have their pockets picked.

For another thing, people were enjoying themselves on Sunday instead of going to church (it would have been widely regarded, in those days, as very nearly blasphemous to suggest that people might enjoy themselves *in* church). As a matter of fact, the urban poor had been staying away from church in droves for some time now. But people who did not live in the midst of them did not always know what they were up to, and if they had, the more militant Sabbatarians would not have thought that a reason for letting things slide. In any event, there was a very strong feeling among the local guardians of the people that Sunday cinemagoing was a Bad Thing. The LCC hastened to forbid it, and prosecuted the Bermondsey Bioscope Company for breach of the condition. The condition was held to be *ultra vires*, but this decision was reversed on appeal. For some years, only a very few towns up and down the country were found to condone this raffish way of going on. At last, however, the LCC relented, and gradually a number of the larger towns followed suit—with cautious regard for piety and decorum, and keeping the Mammon of Unrighteousness at arm's length. A common condition—and later, a legal requirement—was that if films were shown on Sunday, they must not be shown for profit, and the proceeds had to go to charity; they also had to be seemly in character, not just any old piece of sensational Saturday night mayhem. The ruthless and greedy pursuit of riches at all costs was not unknown sixty years ago, but there seems to have been a widespread feeling that it was not merely unattractive but wrong—a sort of Pooh-Bah in reverse: 'I do it, but it revolts me.'

The battle about what was and was not suitable for the Sabbath broke out sporadically for many years and tormented people whose energies might have been expected to be otherwise engaged:

an article in *The Times* just after the First World War said that the question of Sunday entertainment was the most important question to come before the Middlesex County Council for six years. The Cinematograph Exhibitors' Association was accused of running candidates for the approaching local elections whose only policy was 'Restore the Sunday opening of picture houses'. Insults were flung about and much ill temper was generated. Mr F. R. Goodwin, Chairman of the London and Home Counties Branch of the Cinematograph Exhibitors' Association, a most able and public-spirited man, was disconcerted to learn from his opponents' publicity posters that 'a vote for Goodwin was a vote against God'.

In talking about the enthusiasm for Sunday cinema-going in the early years of the century I am talking, of course, exclusively about the English Sunday, not the Welsh and Scottish Sabbath. This was something else again. It still is. Even in these relatively Godless days, the attitude of atheists towards the Deity is akin to the attitude of republicans to the monarch; and it is one thing to disbelieve in monarchy and quite another to be rude to the Queen, as certain university students discovered to their surprise when certain good republican burghers of Stirling refused to serve them in the shops.

But not everybody, then or earlier, could take the Sunday opening of cinemas as seriously as they did another aspect of evil, namely obscenity. Our forbears of those days never felt a need to define obscenity, depravity or corruption. They had no doubt that they knew what obscenity was and that to indulge a taste for it was sinful in man and depraved in woman, and that if you rubbed a child's nose in it you would go straight to hell and serve you right. This was not as wrong-headed as it may seem to most people today. They were still too close, not merely to the prudishness of prosperous Victorians, but also to the justifiable anxiety in which that prudishness had its roots: fear for the welfare of young children in a world where gross and physically unclean prostitution was rife and little girls of thirteen were often corralled into brothels against their will. By contrast, a slow and sheltered growth to maturity seemed to the middle classes most devoutly to be wished, not only for their own children, but for everybody else's too.

It was therefore with some alarm that the trade and the licensing authorities saw the advent from Germany and France of some films which Mr Brooke Wilkinson, Secretary of the newly formed Association of Kinematograph Manufacturers, later stigmatized as un-English. Little was said in the Press, or indeed anywhere else, about this sinister development, for it was not fit to be discussed in polite society. But from other sources it appears that one of the chief un-English activities complained of was the removal by females, as slowly and seductively as possible, of some or all of their clothes, though to be sure it was not possible to do anything very slowly on the silent screen. All were agreed that this sort of thing must be discouraged and that there ought to be, if not exactly a law about it, at any rate some sort of sanction of which the less reputable showmen would feel obliged to take some heed.

Another—mercifully rare—problem was buried deep and not talked about much because it brought shame and grief to everyone concerned. Once in a long time a child died who almost certainly would not have died if he had not gone to the pictures. Here is the sad story of the last hours in the life of Alfred John Rogers, aged eleven, of Anngrave Street, Shoreditch. On the first Saturday in July 1910, he and his mates went to a picture show. One of the short films which they saw sounds very much like *The Black Hand*, mentioned in Nevill March Hunnings' book *Film Censors and the Law* as having been complained of by a local resident when it was shown in East London. In this film, a gangster intimidates a mother by standing her child on a chair with a noose round his neck and threatening to pull the chair away. After his visit to the pictures, young Alfred and his friends played in the street till 10 p.m., when he came in and his parents went out to do the shopping, and quite probably to go to the pub, which would not, then, have closed till midnight. He asked them to bring him some fish for his supper. Just before midnight, they came home. Alfred had not been left in the house alone: the house was probably bursting with other people, and in any case there must have been at least one other family, for when the parents asked where Alfred was an unnamed little girl said 'He's in there', nodding at a bedroom door. And so indeed he was, hanging from a rope behind the door, dead. There was no suggestion that the child was of a nervous or melancholy disposition, no conceivable reason why he should deliberately have taken his own life. There was only one unusual thing, in a poor part of London in 1910, about the way he spent his Saturday, and that was his death and the manner of it. Society may have been guilty, as the current cant phrase goes, but the immediate cause of the lethal experiment was 'the cinematograph show', and once is too often.

Another thing about which all honest citizens and many dishonest ones were fully agreed was that children ought not to be encouraged to steal. By now, a good many boys who were brought before the courts on charges of theft were saying that they got the idea at the pictures. These cases were widely reported under such headings as 'The Cinematograph and Juvenile Crime', or 'Cinematograph blamed for Boy's Downfall'. Some magistrates, and some Chief Constables, believed the boys, but many did not, holding that children who did not mind stealing would not mind lying about it if they thought that this would get them more lenient treatment. However, a great many members of local licensing authorities took statements of this kind at their face value and advocated such drastic remedies that the exhibitors were afraid for the whole future of the cinema. One such alarming straw in the wind was the notice of a motion put down by Mr St. J. Morrow for a meeting of the LCC to be held on 30 April 1912, that:

> The Council is of the opinion that pictorial representations in cinematograph theatres of breaches of the criminal law of England have a demoralising influence upon boys and girls, who form a large proportion of the audience frequenting the same, and directs the Theatres and Music Halls Committee to bring up to the Council forthwith regulations prohibiting such representations in all such theatres licensed by this Council.

It is fascinating to listen to those rugged individualists the city fathers of 1912. One cannot wonder that Mr McKenna, the Home Secretary, said that he could not see his way to establish an official censorship of films; for not only did the licensing authorities often find themselves at loggerheads with the cinema trade, they differed almost as often and violently with one another, and would no doubt have asserted their independence just as vigorously against the central government. One cannot imagine even Mr Morrow of the LCC lying down meekly under an edict from Whitehall that there should be no more gangster films. Their vigour, independence and occasional waywardness were healthy signs: it is far better to have a too fussy local council than one that does not care. The whole structure of democracy is like a tent, held upright, as if by ropes, by the strains of the determination of opposing factions. If any one substantial section of the community ceases to care and gives up the struggle the whole thing is in danger of collapse. But the variety of fashions in what was considered acceptable film fare was bewildering for exhibitors who were trying to operate on a nation-wide scale and agree a common policy.

One of the things about which the licensing authorities were unpredictable was the question of what was and was not fitting in the way of religious films. The LCC allowed the exhibition of a screen representation of the life of Christ called *From Manger to Cross*; it was even considered likely to be uplifting for the prisoners in Wormwood Scrubs. Liverpool would have none of it: they even defeated an amendment that they should see it before making a decision. The Roman Catholic Archibshop of Liverpool had written a letter testifying to the reverent treatment of the subject. But someone had suggested that the film would cause riots in cinemas. Mr James Thompson said that this was rubbish: hundreds of persons paid to see religious pictures and nobody rioted. Mr Muirhead said that if they allowed this at the Liverpool Hippodrome, the next thing they knew it would become a turn on the music-hall bioscope. Mr Henry Jones said that the 80,000 nonconformists whom he represented opposed these pictures being exploited for nothing but money-making purposes. Mr Sexton said that the nonconformist conscience would not allow anybody to have a conscience but themselves. Mr T. Shaw said that that was a very improper remark to make because several Roman Catholics voted against the resolution. Nobody hit anyone, and an invigorating time was had by all. But the violence of the feelings which were aroused on this and similar occasions may explain why, when the British Board of Film Censors started work a few weeks later, the only ingredient in films—besides nudity— which they were quite certain they would not pass was the 'materialised figure of Christ'. When local opinion can become so hotly incensed, mere advisory bodies had better tread very warily.

It was the Cinematograph Exhibitors' Association who, daunted by all this confusion, and sincerely wishing to preserve the good repute of their cherished family entertainment, passed a resolution 'that a censorship is necessary and advisable', made a plan of procedure and detailed the Association of Kinematograph Manufacturers (whose function in those days was to represent not only the makers of cameras and other equipment for producing and showing films, but the people who actually made the films and who were later called producers and directors) to get on with the job. In November Mr McKenna announced in the House that the manufacturers had agreed to establish an office for the examination of films they proposed to put upon the market and that Mr George Redford had been appointed Censor. He added that while the new arrangement was entirely unofficial, he thought that it 'would do much to protect the public from any risk of the production of objectionable pictures'. The powers of the local authorities and police would remain unchanged.

On 1 January 1913, in his office at 77 Shaftesbury Avenue, Mr George Redford started work. He was not new to this sort of thing, having worked in the Lord Chamberlain's theatre censorship office for many years. The Secretary was Mr Brooke Wilkinson, Secretary of the Kinematograph Manufacturers. The four examiners were wrapped in a veil of anonymity, for which they should have been grateful. The representative of the Inspector of Taxes who deals with one's income tax is not singled out for individual ridicule and abuse, whatever one may think of the outfit as a whole, but it can be quite otherwise with examiners of films, once their identity is known to the outside world.

The final decision on what was fit to be seen by the public was to be taken by Mr Redford himself. As he explained in his inaugural statement to the Press:

> ... it was not his intention to take up an antagonistic attitude towards the film manufacturers, and he hoped to be able to enlist their hearty cooperation. He added that when any portion of a picture did not meet with his approval it would not be his desire to ban the film. He would invite the producer to meet him and endeavour to get such alterations made as would remedy the objectionable or questionable portion.

The manufacturers were not obliged to submit their films to the new board, but it was hoped that they would, and with the powerful

Cinematograph Exhibitors' Association throwing their weight into the project, it was likely that they would in the end. There were two certificates, A and U. The 'Universal' certificate indicated that the film was considered fit for everybody, the A that it was considered fit for public exhibition but more suitable for adults than for children; but there was no power, as yet, to keep the children out, accompanied by an adult or not.

Was everyone satisfied? For a few brief weeks, it would almost seem that everybody was, judging by an enthusiastic article in *The Times* of 9 April 1913. At last, the cat was out of the bag: *everybody*, even Top People, was going to the cinema for purposes of sheer, unadulterated pleasure and relaxation. We, with hindsight, can be glad for them, for the sands were running out fast now.

Not that the anonymous contributor expected it to last. But that was because 'these sudden crazes' don't.

> ... thirty years ago it was croquet, fifteen years ago it was cycling, ten years ago it was roller-skating. ... Nevertheless, whenever it happens, the more thoughtful part of the race becomes alarmed, collects statistics, and wonders what this development, which it chooses to call backsliding, is caused by. We have lately been told that picture palaces are preventing us from going to church, from going to the theatre, from going to public houses, and from reading novels. On the other hand, we may find encouragement in the fact that the number of people who use works of reference is increasing.
>
> ... one may wonder as one walks down the Strand or Oxford Street or Tottenham Court Road why these excessively brilliant doorways which star the pavement at such short distances apart prove so irresistibly attractive. It is true that the management often provide tea for nothing, and the carpets are very thick, and the attendants as finely grown as Royal footmen, and all these things are good; but without any such attractions, when the door is unlit and down a back street, and the seats are hard and the attendants meagre and peremptory, we go—we pay our sixpence, we sit there until the first picture begins to come over again, and directly the programme is changed, which is not as often as it should be, we pay our sixpence and go once more.

But what is the reason of it? Why do we invariably find the

British Bioscope Co.,
Cinematograph Experts
(Pro^{rs}. British Bioscope Institute.)
FOR OPERATING.

5, New Oxford St., London, W.C.

Diploma

This is to Certify that Robert Rawcliffe has this day November 11th 1912 passed his examination as a qualified Electrician Bioscope Operator

J. A. Sewi[?], M.A.B.O.
Wm H. Ruddock, E.E.
Instructors

H. Cohen
Secretary

Remarks:-
Reliable
Industrious
Thoroughly recommended

Projectionist's certificate of proficiency, 1912

A patron counts the cost – cartoon from the Kine Weekly, *1922*

hall full of men and women, old, elderly and young, paying their sixpences, listening intently, going away and coming again? No doubt we are all feeling much the same thing, and we are driven to drop in by some such experience as this.

After trudging for an hour and a half in and out of tubes, shops, omnibuses, hard pavement for the feet, grey sky between the houses, wind blown, with uncharitable people to confront, there comes a moment when it is no longer to be borne. . . . The picture palace offers immediate escape with the least possible expenditure of energy. . . . You are now in the position most comfortable to man—sitting at ease, observing, speculating, ruminating, imagining, with hardly any trouble to yourself. All the work seems to be done for you. The marvellous way in which an illusion, strong enough to defeat circumstances, is created at once, without any effort of imagination, must be attributed chiefly to the fact that the picture moves. You never have time to be bored . . . you are being worked upon, as indifferent music that goes straight to the obvious emotion does work upon one, and made to feel without willing it rather more than is reasonable . . . Moving pictures are simpler, quicker, more direct than the best printed prose can ever hope to be. Whether in this extraordinary greed of the eye we are to see reason for alarm or not, we do not know. We are inclined to expect that the eye in England has been rather cruelly starved. At the present moment, at any rate, it will take anything you choose to give it, as long as it moves quickly and is exactly like life. . . . What the brain does with all this material it is difficult to say. [The writer is inclined to believe that the brain remains quiescent most of the time] . . . It is not life, it is not art, it is not music, it is not literature. Whether, all the same, we are fumbling towards some new form of art which is to have movement and shape, to be like life and yet to be selected and arranged as a work of art, who can say? In the meantime we have a fury for seeing and remain happy, greedy and terribly indiscriminate.

This curious piece of prose gives one much food for thought. Absent-mindedly—in the most literal sense of the word—the anonymous writer has become hooked on the most widespread and enduring addiction of our century, the addiction to watching moving images on a screen, and he only equates it with past crazes. But did Edward VII go roller-skating in 1903? He certainly commanded 'the pictures' to come to Buckingham Palace in 1908, and his mother before him sent for them to Windsor in 1897, and their heirs and successors have maintained the interest which they began. And how many people in Hoxton or Whitechapel were playing croquet in 1883? Already, it seems that the past crazes have been dwarfed into insignificance.

Had English eyes indeed been 'rather cruelly starved'? My first conscious memories are of the Hampshire countryside in 1913, and they still enrich my life. But my cinema-going was then all in the future. Looking back at a less distant past, I do seem to have the impression that my later, town years had been 'rather cruelly starved' of colour before the advent of the colour film, and now I am apt to feel starved of colour when I come back from watching someone else's colour television screen to my own black-and-white. Perhaps our correspondent is just displaying symptoms of the addiction.

But it was quite otherwise for people whose horizons were bounded by the Gorbals, or the East End of London, or the less spectacular drabness of other parts of our towns and cities. To them, with the race memories still alive in them of a cleaner, greener land before the industrial revolution, the starvation was real enough, the assuagement welcome. Can one wonder, in particular, that they fell at once for the wide open spaces of the Western, even though, then, the spaces may have been in reality little more than somebody's five-acre field. Rudimentary Westerns and other equally misleading pictures of the American way of life now became, and remained for many years, the chief ingredient of their film diet. You may say, if you like, as the Imperial Conference said in 1927, that the culture of the British Empire was being disastrously overlaid by an alien culture. On the other hand you could say that we redressed the balance by our most remarkable export, a little Cockney music-hall comedian from the Walworth Road, and that Charlie and the Western between them did much to forge the links that held fast twice in our century, to give a large part of mankind at least a stay of execution of savage tyrannies beyond the worst imaginings of the English-speaking world.

The American film did nothing to cement friendship between 'the Establishment' in this country and their cousins across the sea. But 'the people' viewed the matter in a very different light; their idyllic relationship with Hollywood-America lasted long enough; it lasted till they were brought face to face with some of the more sobering aspects of reality in the Second World War.

But to return to our anonymous correspondent, who tells us that the audience 'listen intently' to the silent films. This is very significant. After all, sound came first. Edison wanted pictures as an accompaniment to sounds, not the other way round. And time and again I find that my oldest friends, the founder-members of the cinema-going public, remember from early childhood not what they actually saw on the screen, but that 'the band played softly' or 'whenever the guns went off, they beat upon the big drum'. And some years later my friend Mary 'heard' the dervishes howling in a film about General Gordon when, as she herself says, they must have been howling on the piano, for there was still no sound. And we are apt to forget, because the early piano accompaniments in the smaller houses were often naïve or irrelevant, how much they did to open the ears of many people who did not normally hear any music, in those days before radio, except a band now and then and the hurdy-gurdy in the street, and perhaps the organ in church. The impact was partly, no doubt, because the pianist was there in the flesh, and his—or more often her—effort was present effort, not, like the exertions of the film actors, crystallized into celluloid, frozen into the past. He was shouted down at last by the radiogram, and by the clamour of the sound film after that, but in his day he was at best revered, at worst subjected to the sort of affectionate mockery that one reserves for old and trusted friends.

Is our writer being unfair to the quality of what he has seen? Almost certainly not. There was little 'art of the film' yet. If he was wrong, he was wrong in company with all the leading dramatic critics of the world, for serious artistic assessment of 'the pictures' was still virtually unknown outside the specialist magazines for film-makers, mainly American, and the word 'cinéaste', imported from France where it originally meant any kind of film technician, was not found necessary in its secondary sense of 'devotee of the art of the film' until the middle of the twenties. His doubtful verdict 'Art may yet come of this', at a time when *Birth of a*

Nation had not yet risen above the Western horizon, was no more out of true than the average long-range weather forecast and with less to go on.

Perhaps he is being a little unfair to himself. There does seem to have been a sneaking sense of shame—though not as much as there is today—at the self-indulgent escapism of taking the weight off one's feet and ceasing from mental strife. Our correspondent knew best whether he spent too much of his time in this way. But it is certain that, at the time of this article, there were millions of his fellow-countrymen who did *not* spend too much of their time in this way and for whom the experience was highly therapeutic—though not, of course, in the picture palaces he is talking about, the ones that charged sixpence a seat and had afternoon shows on an ordinary working day.

An interesting feature of the afternoon's entertainment is the free cup of tea. This was never the general rule, and it was magical when it happened. There has always been a kind of magic in so-called free gifts. And it has been clear from the outset that addiction to watching a screen induces hunger and thirst: look at the boom in recent years in 'television pre-prepared meals' and the tendency of any housewives who do not like the commercials to use the break as a convenient opportunity of running out to make a cup of tea. At the very beginning of the century's new addiction, as early as 1908, other top people besides royalty had been indulging a furtive liking for it and, tea being as *Kine Weekly* says, 'a necessary part of a shopping expedition', the grand ladies who shopped in Piccadilly had been slipping into the New Egyptian Hall for a shillingsworth of dainty tea and living pictures. Meanwhile, in the 'penny gaffs' the patrons brought oranges for their refreshment; later on there were crisps, and in really opulent houses the occupants of the boxes could have tea and cakes brought in, and everywhere the traffic in ice-cream flourished exceedingly and became an important part of the economics of the cinema trade. In the biggest and most important cinemas a regular complex of tea lounges, coffee rooms and restaurants sprang up round the auditorium.

In the fifties and sixties the eating habit was still going strong. In the course of my work as an examiner of films at the British Board of Film Censors I had occasion to go with a colleague to examine a film version of *The Student Prince* in a West End cinema in the middle of the night, after the evening programme. While the voice of Mario Lanza boomed improbably from the mouth of Edmund Purdom, the cleaners crawled round our feet picking up mountains of polythene wrappers, cardboard boxes and ice-cream cartons, the debris of the feast.

Last and most important, the article has a significant omission: where, in all this, are the children? At school perhaps, but anyway they would not be here—not in the sixpenny cinemas of the West End, unless in ones and twos, accompanied by affluent parents, and some West End theatres did not admit children at all. But in the evenings, after school, or on Saturday afternoons in the East End and in Leeds and Liverpool, Edinburgh and Southampton and Cardiff and Glasgow, there are the children, the mainstay of the audience. And are *they* happy? There can be more than one opinion about this. Three days later, in the correspondence columns, Canon Rawnsley, a doughty campaigner against the cinema, falls upon our writer with a cry of rage:

> ... As to our happiness, I cannot agree. Those of us who know what a large proportion of the spectators are children between four and fourteen, and that before these children's greedy eyes with heartless indiscrimination horrors unimaginable are in many of the halls presented night after night, are the reverse of happy. Terrific massacres, horrible catastrophes, motor-car smashes, public hangings, lynchings, badger-bating, bullfights, prize fights, pictures of hell fire and the tortures of the damned, &c., are passed before them, and become such realities that they cannot sleep at night and have been known to implore the policeman to guard them on their way home from 'the horrid man with the beard'.
>
> Those of us who know that these same children, after sitting in the cinematograph hall till eleven o'clock at night, come weary and listless to school the following morning, who also from police and magisterial reports are informed that, while many children become petty pilferers to get pence for admission to the show, others actually begin their downward course of crime by reason of the burglary and pickpocket scenes they have witnessed, cannot help feeling very real alarm. It remains to be seen if Mr Redford, the film censor, can work the change for the better that many film-makers

desire. Meantime I dare to suggest that all who care for the moral wellbeing and education of the child will set their faces like flint against this new form of excitement, shall insist that no children under school age be allowed to go to these shows in the evening unless accompanied by their parents or guardians, and that our civic authorities should be called upon not to license any cinematograph hall that will not undertake to give afternoon shows for children on Saturday afternoons, at which all films will be fit for a child to see.

Truly, a spectacle to make Dickens blench and Fagin rub his hands with glee.

Was this respected church dignitary telling lies? It is most unlikely. No doubt he and his friends between them had seen or read about all the horrors he said the children were seeing. And if the grown-ups had seen them, we may be sure the children had too, for the A certificate at this time was advisory only, and it is not likely that the parents who had let their four-year-olds go out in the streets after dark in the care of an older child—or perhaps even alone—now started to worry because they were at the pictures instead, or knew or cared about a category letter displayed at the beginning of a film. In the poorer districts of our cities and big towns virtually all the children were going to the pictures. And this, of course, included the children who stole as well as the children who did not steal—probably a higher proportion of the children who stole, since they, on the whole, came from the worse and more overcrowded homes and had slower-witted and more neglectful parents.

The truth is that the huge canvas of the cinema scene of 1913 is an amalgam of every sort of entertainment, after the manner of *Comic Cuts* and Hieronymus Bosch and Ouida and Dante's *Inferno* and Ethel M. Dell and Jack London and an off-moment on the Halls. One cannot say that all these ingredients are equally suitable for children. And as the audience included the huge majority of the children of the poor, you can find evidence in support of anything you hope to prove, and the deductions drawn will continue to be varied and contradictory.

At the London sessions in October, when a boy was convicted of theft, the prosecutor pointed out that one of the houses broken into belonged to a cinematograph proprietor and said, in effect, that it served him right.

I have no means of knowing whether it served this particular cinematograph proprietor right. But a little booklet on how to run a cinema, published in 1911 by *Kine Weekly*, makes it clear that the better sort of proprietor was a paragon of probity and public spirit by the standards of his day. He was concerned for 'the labouring classes', though he had a romantic longing for the approbation and patronage of 'the carriage trade'. He was firm, but kind to his staff, especially the female staff (who, he said, in subordinate positions like that of cashier, were not only cheaper than men, but more reliable, so that you would do well to pay a cashier £1 a week for handling all that money, even though you could get one for 12s. 6d.). Any tendency to flirt with the patrons must be discouraged, and a second offence must mean instant dismissal; but those who showed themselves trustworthy must be trusted. You might even deck the female attendants in alluring fancy dress, as *vivandières*, or after the style of Marie Antoinette; but on the whole the preference is for something more sober and less provocative, a decent black dress, with white cap and apron. As for the films, good quality is to be preferred at all times to 'trashy comics' (which the carriage trade will not accept anyway), and a special effort must be made to make the Sunday programme appropriate to the day, otherwise how will one still the outcry against the Sunday opening of picture houses? In all this one can see that rectitude was backed by self-interest. But if this was the sort of sober citizen who deserved to be robbed—well, so did most of the other business men of the years just before the First World War.

The more excitable section of public opinion continued to think otherwise, however. In Sutton Coldfield in February of the following year a number of lads who had been convicted of a series of thefts were bound over not to enter a picture theatre for twelve months. The Chairman of the Bench said that the town had been made notorious as a den of young thieves and shopkeepers had been terrorized. The local branch of the Women's Temperance Association urged that all pictures showing 'violence and wrongdoing' should be banned. The Bench kept its head and contented itself with hoping that exhibitors would be careful what they showed and would provide afternoon programmes for children.

In the same month the British Board of Film Censors presented its first annual report and the view was expressed 'that the existence of the board had had a salutary effect in gradually raising the standard of subject, and eliminating anything repulsive or objectionable to the good taste and better feelings of British audiences'.

In May came the inauguration of the Educational Cinematograph Association. The sponsors concede 'that the cinematograph has come to stay, that its attractions are within the reach of all, and its continual variety ensures vitality'.

They think that little good has come of it yet, but that if it inspires 'youthful evildoers' it may yet inculcate more elevating thoughts. They add a word of praise for 'the censorship', which, they say, 'has done much to eliminate the objectionable film, but there are other subjects . . . which, while they can be in no way classified as indecent, deal with matters which it is not altogether desirable that the youthful mind should visualize too vividly'. With the word 'objectionable' we seem to be back with our old problem of identifying the 'un-English', or, to put it bluntly, mildly obscene, film without soiling our lips with any such un-English word.

In July, at the Canterbury Diocesan Conference, the Rev. H. E. Oliver proclaimed that 'the ineffectiveness of the censorship as at present exercised was shown in scenes which had depicted some aspects of relationships between the sexes. Anything like steadiness and work was scouted and made to appear ridiculous'. He said, however, that 'it was most important that those who thought there was a case for serious research into the matter should not let it be known that they were out for the suppression of the people's pleasures'.

Probably what he meant to say was 'should not let it be *thought*' rather than '*known*'. But it seems likely from the general tenor of his remarks that if this was a slip of the tongue it was a Freudian slip, that he was one of a minority of churchmen who were nervous of this new entertainment, which belonged first and foremost to 'the ordinary man in the street'. The more humane and wise ones realized, as the Jewish community had realized from the beginning, that it was not the part of true religion and virtue to try to beat lawful amusements: the answer was to join them and hope to provide any leaven of righteousness that might be lacking. Such was the Rev. Thomas Horne of Syresham, one of the pioneers of the early travelling showmen; or the Roman Catholic Archbishop of Liverpool, who had said that it was not necessarily irreverent to bring the Gospel story to the screen; such, too, was a dedicated

Methodist layman, already old enough for the Western Front, who first came into the motion picture business some twenty years later from evangelical motives. It is fashionable to accuse of hypocrisy any Christian whose achievements have fallen short of his aspirations, even if his hopes have been as high as those of J. Arthur Rank; and if, in addition, he had made a lot of money—well, we have been told that with God's help it is not impossible for a rich man to get into the kingdom of heaven, but we know better. However, in the business of bringing cinematograph films to the mass of the people, the long-range alternatives are to succeed as dramatically as the Rank Organization or finally fade out of the picture—there is no middle way. A state-run industry would not be expected to make a profit, but on the other hand, except for propaganda purposes in a totalitarian state, it would never get the sort of subsidy which is obtainable for the material necessities of life and it would be among the first casualties in hard times. Not every state will opt for guns instead of butter, but every state will assuredly give them preference over motion pictures, and the people need some fun if they are to keep going in times of slump or war—the times which were now coming upon the world.

On 2 July 1914, on the same page of *The Times* as Mr Oliver's unguarded remark about the people's pleasure, there appears an advertisement which states that 'The domestic servant problem is one of the most serious problems of the present day'. That day the temperature at Henley was eighty-eight in the shade. The *Daily Mirror* gave pride of place to the weather, the *Daily Mail* to 'the Great Thames Festival', while the *Evening News* made sport with a speech by Mr Philip Snowdon about the tea duty. The *Daily Mail*, in its second leader, did say that 'it would be deplorable if the dastardly outrage at Sarajevo should be allowed to have a diplomatic complication as a sequel', but on the whole the London papers were disinclined to look further afield than the imminent danger of civil war in Ulster. It was business as usual as Britian sleep-walked towards the abyss. Less than five weeks later, she toppled over the edge.

2
In Time of War

By 1916 Theda Bara had become a star; so had John Barrymore; the début of Will Rogers came in 1918. A few films to remember are *Birth of a Nation*, *Intolerance*, the British documentary *Battle of the Somme*, John Barrymore's *Raffles*, Theda Bara's *Under Two Flags*, Chaplin's *Easy Street* and *Shoulder Arms*, *Cabinet of Dr Caligari*.

2
In Time of War

With heady anticipation, like children outside a cinema, the young men jostled to get into the war—to let off steam, to teach the Hun a lesson, and to be home by Christmas. For their brief spell in training camps in England they were bored and lonely; the local picture palace was a great relief. It was universally agreed that this aspect of the cinema, if no other, was a good thing; some local authorities were even persuaded by the military to agree to Sunday opening for the sake of the troops. Being more lenient about the opening of picture houses was the least the local authorities and the military could do to make life more tolerable, not only for the troops but for everyone else, for they had been swift to curtail the opening hours of public houses under new powers conferred upon them in the first month of the war by the Defence of the Realm Act and other legislation specially designed to control the sale of intoxicating liquor. The seaports were the first to feel the drought: by the end of August 1914 all the 900 inns in Portsmouth had to close by 9 p.m. In Sheerness they all had to close between 7 and 8 p.m., after which civilians were let in again but the military were not.

Back home on embarkation leave, the soldiers took their

sweethearts or wives to the picture palace rather than to the music hall. For the relative darkness is friendly to lovers, though how much use they make of their opportunities in public depends upon the conventions of their day and of the social circles in which they move.

As fast as the soldiers went overseas, there were other soldiers to fill the picture palaces—some newly mobilized, others, 'our Colonials' as they were called, arriving in transit from their native lands, lonely and at a loss, regarded with some suspicion by the native-born, who had hardly yet got over their peace-time habit of thinking of even British strangers in uniform as brutal and licentious soldiery on the look-out for an opportunity of corrupting innocent girls.

Meanwhile, the soldiers' younger brothers had the chance, at fourteen, of doing a man's work for a man's pay, and one of the ways in which they spent their new-found riches was by going to the pictures oftener than ever. So, too, did the school-children, for in the less easy-going and over-crowded homes, where dad had sometimes put his foot down about too frequent evenings out, dad was no longer there. Sometimes the mothers accompanied their children, to take their minds off their loneliness and fears. The young wives, and later the young widows, came by themselves, or with their babies in arms: no good sitting at home and brooding, and if people's lives have perforce been spent in crowds, it is usually to crowds that they turn for comfort, rather than to the desert place apart.

In 1916, the war widow Mrs Field, on a visit from the country to her sister in London, took her six-year-old elder daughter and her four-year-old only son to see their first film, a topical yarn about the unmasking of a spy. I cannot pretend that I remember anything whatever about this occasion, but my brother remembers everyone laughing when, at the dénouement, he remarked with loud and calm satisfaction, 'Now he's going to give it him hot!' After that we went home to the country and our cinema-going ceased for about four years. But my cousin in Bognor, the same age as myself, soon started going regularly to her local, reading out the captions in a loud voice for the benefit of a less erudite little girl.

One way and another, people were now going to the pictures in greater numbers than ever before: by 1916 the annual attendances had greatly overtopped the billion mark. The most popular price for a seat was threepence, but plenty of seats were sold at a penny, and there was no lack of opulent patrons who would spend as much as a shilling a time.

Things were not quite as they used to be, of course. The 'attendants as finely grown as royal footmen' had discarded their eye-catching uniforms for khaki and whether we shall see them again no one knows. Their places had been taken by those unfit for military service, by old men and by girls. When conscription came in, there was little deferment for the people about the picture palaces. The advertisements in the trade press tell their own tale:

> Wanted . . . smart, experienced manager (ineligible for the Army) . . . electrical operator (ineligible) . . . Electrician wanted for Cinema, £2.15 per week. Must have practical experience of gas and electricity and able to give first class projection. Ineligible for military service; steady and reliable man preferred.

In the same issue of *Kine Weekly* we learn that 'Mr Seddon of Salford has taken the wise course of teaching Miss Thorley, his cashier, how to manipulate the projector and generator. . . . At many theatres in the North women operators have been appointed and are giving satisfaction. The question of sex seems to have faded away like mist before the morning sun, and trust with confidence is the rule.'

And, 'The Imperial Playhouse in Kings Road, Chelsea, S.W., just now presents the unique spectacle of a lady commissionaire. This comely damsel, armed with an ebony wand, performs all the various duties of a commissionaire or liveried attendant.'

While these developments are approved, the author of 'Weekly Notes' in the same paper a month later angrily repudiates the suggestion made by *The Star* that one of the professions newly opened to women is film viewing. 'Personally', says the writer, 'I do not regard the decorative sex at a trade show as a business proposition.'

Even with the women pressed into service, there were not enough attendants to please the people who thought that every patron who was not watched would either accost somebody or behave improperly in the back row. The shortage was so acute that some of the remoter rural houses had to close down altogether. But this did not mean that the depleted country population was deprived of the pictures: it just gave bigger opportunities to the remaining travelling showmen. Says *Kine Weekly* in April 1916:

> When the question of repopulating the deserted countryside is taken up—as it must be—after the war, statesmen and politicians will have to take into account the gigantic influence of the travelling showman in helping to make tolerable the life of Farmer Giles and his assistants. Rural depopulation would have been far more complete than it is but for the entertainment provided by the travelling kinema, which has proved an efficient substitute for the pleasures and attractions of town life.

And the number of picture palaces in the country as a whole did not decline much. Luxury building was no longer permitted, and Mr Sol Levy's Futurist Cinema in Birmingham, which was to be the eighth wonder of the world, had to languish half-finished till 1919. But one could revert to the old practice of adapting any existing building that could be brought up to the required standard of safety without too much expense.

It need hardly be said that to the people who were alarmed before about the growing popularity of the cinema, this was a very unsatisfactory state of affairs, the more so as the populace had been asked to work harder and save money for the war effort. A clergyman (prudently signing himself only 'A Black Country Vicar'), wrote to *The Times* on 5 July 1915:

> If the War Loan is to have any chance with the 'working classes', at least in the Midlands, the compulsory closing of picture palaces will become an absolute necessity. They are probably a more serious menace to the nation now than even drink.

This provoked an angry reply from Mr H. W. Ledger of the Royal Picture House at Egremont, Cheshire, pointing out that picture palaces had never ceased to stimulate recruiting, to make appeals for the Red Cross and the National Relief Fund, to help

```
        KEEP THIS TICKET.
   It will remind you that the Unique and Startling
                 Attractions,
   THE BEGINNING & THE END
            and  TRILBY
              Are at the
   CARLTON THEATRE, Saltley,      2122
      Monday, November 7th,
          And during the Week.
   The World's Weirdest Creation—Vide Press.
     Mr. A. B. Mackay as SVENGALI.
```

```
TRILBY                                      TRILBY
        What every Woman ought to Know.
        THE BEGINNING & THE END
               A VISIT TO THE
              CARLTON THEATRE,
           Monday, November 7th
              And during the Week,
         Will reveal the Great Moral Lesson,
          The essence of dramatic art.
                                —Vide Press.
```

☛ NOTICE.

SUMMONS TO APPEAR.

District of
Saltley
To Wit.

To all His Majesty's Loving Subjects in the District of Saltley.

WHEREAS complaint has this day been made before the undersigned, one of His Majesty's subjects appointed to provide amusement for the inhabitants of this District, that divers persons have been seen walking up and down the Roads, Streets, Alleys, Courts, and other thoroughfares of the District, not knowing where to spend their time or find amusement.

You are therefore commanded, in His Majesty's name, to be and appear on **THURSDAY and FRIDAY, OCTOBER 27th and 28th,** at the **CARLTON THEATRE,** in this District, it being for your own benefit to witness the production of the Powerful Domestic Drama, entitled "THE STOWAWAY," by TOM CRAVEN. You are to appear with the current coin of the realm, or cheques to that effect, that you may be conducted accordingly by the Officers in Waiting to your seat, to answer the charge of wandering abroad when such a night's entertainment is provided for you.

And, should you fail to appear, you will be dealt with according to law.

Given under my hand and seal this 1st day of January, 1912.

(Signed)
VICTOR DU CANE,
General Manager.

'Throwaways and Striking Novelties' – publicity suggestions from the Kine Weekly's *handbook,* How to Run a Picture Theatre

'A Few Typical Fronts', from How to Run a Picture Theatre

with propaganda designed to lure people into the munitions factories. He suggested acidly that 'money might be saved by abolishing the collecting box'.

A representative of Pathé Frères, also taking up the cudgels on behalf of the much maligned picture house, and quoted in *Kine Weekly* in March 1916, cannot be considered an unbiased witness, but all the same, he was there; and a weakness of many critics of the cinema, then as now, is that on their own admission they do not go. And he says of a cinema in Salford:

> I shall not forget the sight which presented itself to me. Hundreds upon hundreds of the toiling population of Salford were gathered together for the purpose of enjoyment and recreation. Man and wife, sons and daughters, thronged the auditorium. The man fresh from work, and the woman from the loom, sat together free from care for a couple of hours, so that the toil of the morrow could be faced with renewed courage and hope.

But the angry accusations went on. In February 1916 a gentleman, prudently only signing himself 'Manufacturer', complained of absenteeism in his London factory on Monday afternoons—the girls *would* go to the picture house. 'No one grudges the relaxation which these entertainments afford to the labouring classes,' but... but...

And *The Times did* grudge the relaxation: it said so, the very next day, in a peevish article headed 'At the Cinema—A World of Inanity'. Here, the cinema stands arraigned for misinformation, false values, 'a degree of stupidity amounting to immorality', and also odd social manners, which may well have seemed less odd to the people of Bethnal Green than to the people reading their *Times* over breakfast in the Shires or Berkeley Square. For example, '... the American butler ushers in with an affable smile the guest who comes with his luggage in a small handbag, which he takes with him into the drawing-room. Here both his hands are invariably grasped by the hostess...'

The article concludes, in a burst of irritation, 'The cinema has proved that it can do beautiful and useful things, but unless it does them in a rather larger measure it would be as well that the highly explosive substances of which these thousands of miles of celluloid film are made should be employed, not against ourselves, but our enemies'.

It seems that not only were people wasting their money, they were being encouraged to treat the war with unbecoming levity or ignore it altogether. An anonymous 'neutral', distinguished enough to have been invited to contribute a series of articles to *The Times*, complained a year earlier that when, out of curiosity, he went to one of the largest picture theatres:

> ... there was not one film shown to give any idea of the work of the British Army or the British Navy. The whole audience looked forward to the antics of one Charlie Chaplin.
>
> I could not but compare a similar scene at a great picture theatre in Germany, where prices had been lowered and parents are entitled to take their children free; where all soldiers enter free, and all wounded free, in order that the nation may obtain, from ocular demonstration, information on the one national topic—the war. If I may be permitted to say so, the impression created in my mind by the contrast was unpleasant. I am told that there are thousands of these picture theatres in London and in the provinces, in Scotland and Ireland, and that Charlie Chaplin is the idol of millions of your people. The only sign of war was that some of your generals were thrown on the screen, but they received relatively small applause. An English friend of mine explained that the English are not enthusiastic in the matter of loud clapping, but I pointed out that Charlie Chaplin received a positive ovation.

It is only fair to the people at home to add that they *did* want 'documentary' short pictures of the war in progress and of life behind the lines in France—not close shots of horrors, but the sort of thing that a non-combatant could usually obtain. And as to the relative entertainment value of Charlie and the generals, the fighting men endorsed their opinion: when, in rest billets, they got the chance, their favourite relaxation was a good laugh at the pictures. The poet might call for

> no more jokes in music-halls
> To mock the riddled corpses round Bapaume,

In Time of War

but to the ordinary people of Britain this made no sense at all. This strange race, called by our 'neutral' the most phlegmatic in Europe except the Dutch, had been, so to speak, carriers of poetry through the ages—they had got poets though they were none—and they had in their bones a deeper and more ancient wisdom,

> These deeds must not be thought
> After these ways—so it will make us mad.

With a sound instinct, and with an artistic flair quite beyond their usual compass, they turned to Charlie, in whose presence, as with nobody else, they could be one people, annihilating in a great wave of laughter the gulfs between rich and poor, between 'highborn' and 'low-born', between those who had gone to fight and those who were left at home. For 'laughing at Charlie' was really the only experience common to Britons once close to one another and now on opposite sides of the narrow sea.

As for a few extraordinary people of Britain among the guardians of Church and State and of the parish pump, they were caught up no less in the general storm and strain. They conceived it to be their duty to look after others, and there was no one to look after *them*. In anxiety and bereavement they beat about them and made more dust than ever, as a woman who has lost a beloved relative will sometimes seek relief in turning out a room. How else to explain the nervous intensity with which, in the middle of the most terrible war in history, they applied themselves to the pressing problem of revising the censorship of cinematograph films.

They very nearly succeeded in bringing about the state censorship which the State, in reality, was reluctant to undertake, knowing that no state which undertakes this function can escape being accused of political censorship. They would probably have succeeded, but for the death, late in 1916, of Mr George Redford, the Chairman of the British Board of Film Censors. Those who knew Mr Redford say that he was an admirable choice for the job, but he had been ill for some time, and though effective control had passed into the forceful hands of Mr Brooke Wilkinson, this was no time for the outfit to be without a titular head known to the world at large and able to hold his own among other public figures. Mr Redford's successor, the Irish journalist and Member of Parliament T. P. O'Connor, was very well able to hold his own, and there seems to have been a feeling that he ought to be given a chance to show what he could do. Also, the new Home Secretary, Sir George Cave, wanted the job even less than Mr McKenna had wanted it. The British Board of Film Censors as originally constituted survived by the skin of its teeth.

But to say that the Board had the confidence of the more rabid critics of the cinema would be an over-statement, and even if it had enjoyed this confidence, there was as yet nothing it could do about films considered unsuitable for children except, by means of the A certificate, advise their parents to keep them out.

And even if the films could be made blameless, what about the picture palaces themselves? Legislation had controlled the fire hazard, but were people asphyxiating themselves with all that tobacco smoke? And were the cinemas warm enough? And above all, were they light enough when the film was showing?

Which brings us back to the twin manifestations of what they called 'the social evil'—soliciting and improper behaviour, clearly easier, for those who wished to indulge in them, now that so many of the attendants had gone to the wars. People who thought that England began and ended with London, and who had barely heard of Scotland and Wales—let alone Ireland, which was no less the legislators' responsibility then—were greatly concerned about 'the social evil', which in fact, as far as it existed at all, was mainly confined to London, the preferred stamping-ground of prostitutes, now finding life in the music-halls rather too difficult and looking for somewhere else (not, for choice, the cold and rainy streets) to ply for hire. Young girls up from the provinces, without money, far from their relations and friends, fallen on evil days, met young men, newly arrived with the forces from overseas, far from the restraining influence of *their* relations and friends, and with their service pay burning a very small hole in their pockets. One could not say that it was easy, in wartime London, to keep all the picture palaces fit for children to live in (as, after school hours, some of the children very nearly did). One could only say that the powerful Cinematograph Exhibitors' Association were aware of the difficulties and were doing their best.

They did their best now. Not for the first time in their brief history, they, with the rest of the trade, took the bull by the horns. They extended to the National Council for Public Morals the invitation for which it had long been hankering, to institute a committee of inquiry into the state of the cinema. This admirable body is now defunct—void for uncertainty rather than for having outlived its usefulness, unless you equate 'morals' with 'sexual abstinence', which was rather too sweeping for sensible people even then. Most of the members of the Council were sensible people, and even if they had not been, a committee of inquiry would have been a very good idea. Nothing needs to come of such a committee; indeed, it is not unusual for its findings to be completely ignored. But it is a wonderful means of letting off steam and giving the more wrong-headed extremists the 'platform' which, sometimes, is all they really need to keep them happy.

The committee included representatives of the trade, the local authorities, the churches and education. Their names would now mean little to the public at large, with two exceptions—the very first Chief Scout and Dr Marie Stopes, an unlikely juxtaposition. They both seem to have kept pretty quiet, and we do not know them any better at the end of the proceedings than we did at the beginning. But the record of the committee's deliberations does give us a very vivid impression of some of the people who gave evidence, and indeed of many facets of life in the poorer parts of the towns and cities of Britain at war. Country life comes into the picture very seldom, except in the most general terms: the real boom in picture palaces in the remoter villages did not come till later, and a good many country people were still out of reach of any pictures except those shown by the travelling showmen, who seem to have escaped the notice of most of the critics on this occasion. And in town and country alike the anxious sociologists were not greatly worried about the amusements of the prosperous and law-abiding middle class, who were known to be waging the war with fervour and looking after their children with fussy thoroughness. And, as usually happens with the reports of committees of inquiry, we get a much deeper insight into the minds of the guardians than of those they are hoping to guard. But this is none the less a good survey, and wide-ranging, thanks largely to the Bishop of Birmingham, a very shrewd and well-mannered chairman, who does not obtrude his own personality but makes sure that his witnesses have a chance to say what is in their minds. The people with most in their minds that is really germane to the issue are, not unnaturally, the trade representatives, several of whom, besides giving evidence, are members of the committee themselves. Of these, the key figure is Mr Newbould, Chairman of the Cinematograph Exhibitors' Association, who really does know the trade from A to Z, having been involved in manufacturing films and being now the head of, among numerous other trade organizations, the first real 'circuit' of picture palaces, Provincial Cinematograph Theatres (which later became part of the Gaumont group, which in its turn became part of the Rank empire, so that his heirs and successors are still in the business today). His activities outside the world of the cinema later included representing the West division of Leyton in Parliament as an Independent Liberal from 1919 to 1922.

From him, and from the other trade representatives, we get a panoramic view of between four and five thousand cinemas up and down the country, each accommodating from one hundred patrons to between three and four thousand. The most palatial cost over £100,000 to build—quite a lot of money, even now—and many included cafés and restaurants. (Could success in the catering trade by people not primarily concerned with catering make for them powerful enemies? the Chairman wanted to know; Mr Newbould agreed that it could.)

The best shape for a cinema (said Mr N. B. Harman) was that of a fan, with the point chopped off to make room for the screen—as like as possible to 'Dr Horton's church at Hampstead', which he considered 'the best building in London'. (This is the Congregational Church in Lyndhurst Road, to which I paid a dutiful pilgrimage. The little elderly caretaker who showed me round said that he took up his duties in 1917. It looked to me as if it would indeed make a very good cinema, but for a good deal of waste space because of the wide pillars in the balcony. But, despite a sharp decline in the size of the congregations, it is still managing to fulfil the purpose for which it was first intended.)

The poorest picture houses, it was agreed, were not what they ought to be, and not what they would have been if the war had not halted renovation and rebuilding. But all agreed that even the humblest and poorest were, since the Cinematograph Act of 1909, as safe as they could be made. And nearly everyone agreed that they were at least adequately ventilated, though the Chief Constable of Guildford, whom we shall meet again, had some harsh things to say on that score.

And anyway, in the poorest houses not less than in the grander ones, about half the population of these islands were voting with their feet, coming to the pictures regularly week in and week out—most of them once a week or more often—to the tune of well over a billion attendances a year. People who did not like what they got were not slow to complain 'with democratic outspokenness', to use the phrase of Mr F. R. Goodwin, Chairman of the London Branch of the CEA. The trade was at pains to emphasize that theirs was the first truly democratic entertainment (Mr Newbould added that he would not have any boxes in his theatres because he considered them snobbish). The exhibitors also pointed out that theirs was the first entertainment to cater, systematically and continually, for children. And children on their own, at that. Unaccompanied children were still the majority of the audience in the more modest cinemas where they could afford to pay the price. And, in a sense, the patrons who were paying least were getting the best service, for they were not only being entertained, they were being looked after as well. Either by local regulation (for example, in London) or through the good will and common-sense of the cinema manager, they were usually seated in blocks of seats specially reserved for them, and in the care of a special attendant.

Mr Newbould conceded that the situation was not perfect, that the war had meant a decline in the number and quality of attendants and that the supervision of children and adults alike in certain parts of the country left something to be desired. But he and his coleagues felt aggrieved—and one can hardly wonder at it—that there were between two and three hundred different sets of conditions for the licensing of cinemas, and that, according to them, 'many of these conditions have nothing to do with safety, and of those that have, many are absurd'.

Mr Newbould's obvious sense of responsibility and unrivalled knowledge of the subject were not without their effect upon the gathering. But even he did not escape censure. His colleague Mr F. R. Goodwin, examined by the Chairman, incurred a reproof, 'I notice that you quote the Chairman of your Association as making a "true and tender remark" when he said that the sight of people linking arms, or with arms round each other's waists, is rather a thing to rejoice to see in a cinema theatre than to be down upon. You accept that?' 'Yes.' 'Most of them, I suppose, are presumed to be people engaged to be married?' 'Yes, we assume that is so.' 'I think that assumption shows a very wide charity on your part.' Mr Newbould recalled the meeting sharply to a sense of reality with the observation '. . . real indecency, of course, goes very much further than that, and I say as a fact that it does not take place in our theatres.'

It was all very well for Mr Newbould to talk like this about his seventy theatres, but what about the rest, many of them with boxes, those dark recesses which, besides being 'snobbish', could be difficult to keep in order? The committee continued to have the gravest misgivings, and strange ideas about the practicability of showing pictures in cinemas as brightly lit as music-halls. It must have been a relief to the exhibitors that professional opinion about the effects of picture-going on the eyes was at any rate against bright lights at right angles to the line of vision.

Otherwise, opinions about eye-strain in cinemas were rather mixed. But the early silent films did not become known as 'the flicks' or 'the flickers' for nothing, and people who did not particularly want to watch them anyway found the flickering hard to bear. My friend Mary, coming of a family who thought the new entertainment somewhat beneath their intellectual dignity, allowed the flickering to induce nausea when as a small girl, she was taken by her mother to see *Sixty Years a Queen*; she would not go again for a long time, but when she was finally persuaded to take a look at *The Gold Rush* with 'this Charlie Chaplin that everyone's talking about' she laughed so much that she quite forgot to suffer from vertigo.

I believe that, if one's eyes have any weakness, much watching of films or television does find it out. My own slight astigmatism stood up quite well to everyday use, but the brief craze in the early fifties for 3-D films, viewed through little pairs of spectacles with one red and one green eyepiece, quite defeated them, and I had to take to proper spectacles for film-viewing. The examiners of the British Board of Film Censors in 1917 said that they did not think that viewing films every day did their eyes any harm, but all the same, one of them had bought a pair of tinted spectacles.

The senior examiner attended the Committee of Inquiry, clad in his cloak of anonymity and the only adult witness to appear in the minutes as 'Mister Blank'. Mister Blank comported himself with suitable reticence and we do not learn much about him except that his new Chief, Mr T. P. O'Connor, considered him to be 'a gentleman in manner and mind'. Mister Blank himself was not present at the time of this encomium. Of the other examiners, Mr O'Connor said that one had just been called up 'for some sort of military service' and as there was no Irishman or Catholic among the remaining three, he thought it right to appoint an Irish Catholic. This left the Irish Catholics not badly represented on the very small Board, Mr O'Connor being one himself, and it was doubtless in those early days that a rumour sprang up that the Board was Roman Catholic-dominated, an idea which remained current long after the last Catholic member of the staff had departed some thirty-three years later. Besides Mister Blank and the Irish Catholics there was 'a fairly experienced man of the world' and finally 'a man I do not know anything about, except that he is a sort of Joan of Arc, that is, vigorous of criticism of anything approaching indecorum'. It is to be hoped that Joan of Arc and the fairly experienced man of the world had a restraining influence upon one another.

The four gentlemen (it will be noted that there were no ladies) had at least two things in common: they were gluttons for hard work and spartan in enduring discomfort. For according to their chief they viewed films all day during five days out of the seven, working late into the evening 'when the boats came in from America'. 'They sit in a rather small and not very comfortable room, and there are two films exhibited simultaneously. One film is examined by two examiners on the right, and another by two examiners on the left.' Mr O'Connor added that each pair could easily see both films, so that in any case of doubt about either film they all consulted and reached a unanimous conclusion.

This is a very daunting prospect and I find it difficult to believe. In my experience it is quite hard enough to examine one film at a time, though I do concede that the sound film of today, with its glorious many-coloured blood and guts, is a rather different proposition. Although Mr O'Connor had been active in the film world for several years, I am inclined to think that he did not yet know much about the highly specialized field into which he had so recently strayed. It should be added that he became a most conscientious Chairman and it is said of him that when he was ill he had a portable screen brought to his bedside so that he could give the final verdict on films involving changes in policy.

Mr O'Connor had all the makings of a television personality, if only he had lived at the right time. So, too, had another colourful character who gave evidence to the Committee, Mr J. Legge, Director of Education of the City of Liverpool. He was often wrong-headed, sometimes shrewdly brilliant, never dull. He conceded that grown-up people must have their amusements, of which the cinema was the chief. But his views about its effect on children were so extreme that they gave aid and comfort to his enemies rather than to his friends. He thought that there might be something to be said for educational and informative films for children—but not much. According to him, the place of films in education had been over-rated: it was in order for education to be made interesting, but it should not be exciting, and he thought that even the importance of interesting the pupils had been valued too highly of late years. If children must be in the picture palace at all, the best thing was to show them films about possible careers; the worst fare was 'not only films depicting crime, immorality and fraud, but also scenes of love-making, vulgar buffoonery, horse-play, practical joking of a mischievous type and successful imposture, which is none the less to be condemned if it is supposed to be comic'. In short, the best thing to do was to keep the children out of the picture palaces altogether, as far as it lay in the power of the local authority. He realized that this was not completely practicable, but Liverpool did at least manage to keep unaccompanied children out after 6.30 p.m. The trouble with this, of course, was that adults who were not their parents or guardians were too easily persuaded to take them in: the principal of one school in the city found that 40 per cent of the children from his school who attended any cinema show in one week in 1916 were 'smuggled in' in this way.

If unaccompanied children persisted in going to the afternoon shows, there was another shot in Mr Legge's locker: where the price of admission was twopence or less, then the performance should be deemed to be a children's show, and *then* printed synopses and programmes should be sent to the police for approval not less than twenty-four hours before the show, thus ensuring, one may hope, that no more than a proper quota of 'vulgar buffoonery', etc., was included. Mr Legge quite realized that he was on a sticky wicket legally with some of these precautions, that the purpose of the Cinematograph Act really was to ensure public safety in the strictly physical sense. But he did not care, because

'The difficulty in the way of regulations such as these . . . has been met in Liverpool by attaching them to a music licence'.

What the people needed, he concluded, was above all better housing, so that they would not want to spend so much time outside their homes, and next, better public houses, to which they should then be allowed to take their children, it being important that families should spend their leisure together.

By now, it seems, Mr Legge had set everybody by the ears and was really enjoying himself. He stood up happily and outrageously to a barrage of angry questions. Was he aware, when he spoke of informative films for children, that almost every filmable industry had been filmed and shown throughout the country several times? 'Several times!' he replied. 'It should be shown continually; there should be no show without it.' 'Do you know that the films showing the sailor's life have been shown so frequently that mothers complain that their boys run away to sea?' 'No, that is new to me, but if it is true I am pleased.' 'Is it not a fact that in the music licences they prohibit the use of brass instruments?' 'That I do not know, but I would rather they prohibited brass instruments than string instruments.' 'You are, I am sure, with me when I say that the working classes spend more on drink than they do on rent?' 'I believe that is true.' 'You say . . . "Healthy means for indoor recreation for children and their elders might be found in reformed public-houses". May I ask you very definitely whether you mean the non-alcoholic house or the continental café?' 'No, I distinctly mean the place where you can get alcohol.' 'Have you seen Charlie Chaplin yourself?' 'In a film, yes.' 'Did it strike you as being vulgar and stupid?' 'Yes, but I enjoyed it very much.' 'Have you seen him a second time?' 'Yes.' 'Did you enjoy him as much as ever?' 'Yes, I have only seen him twice.' 'Can you imagine the cinematograph or the author of cinematograph writing plots with the love interest cut out?' 'No, but I think it is very bad for children to see an adult love-making on the film.' 'You would not press the point to cut it out and therefore spoil the cinema?' 'No, but I would have them very closely watched, particularly the scenes of love-making in the kitchen between the policeman and the cook.'

Another rather gloomy assessment of the place of the cinema in the lives of children came from Miss Vickers of the LCC Care Committees, attached to a school in Tower Street, Seven Dials (*not* the darkest East End, but among the bright lights of theatre land, only few yards from where the Cambridge Theatre now stands). 'The Blank Blank Blank', she said (offending cinemas, like offending films and the examiners of the British Board of Film Censors, were shrouded in anonymity) 'was very rowdy the whole time. A man was walking about trying to keep the children quiet, and there was a great commotion at the beginning of the second performance owing to those outside fighting to get in.' 'Was there no adequate provision for keeping order?' 'They were shouting—it was like Babel.'

One can well understand how Miss Vickers felt. But one can also drink in the heady draughts of anticipation and know how the customers felt. You do not fight to get into hell. One can quite understand, also, the temptation, to which certain showmen succumbed, to accommodate three children to every two seats. The committee was greatly concerned about the herding together of large numbers of children, as one or two of them had received reports of indecency by older children to younger ones. But such incidents must have been rare, for Mr Newbould himself was obviously astonished as well as horrified: he had heard of the occasional case of indecency by an adult to a child, but by a child to a child—never.

A few children, boys and girls from schools in the London area, had actually been invited to speak for themselves on this occasion, which was a novel idea for those days. They, on being asked if the boys were ever 'rude' to the girls, obviously had no idea what was in the questioners' minds. The consensus of opinion was that, yes, sometimes the boys threw orange-peel at the girls, knocked their hats off or pulled their hair—but no, the girls did not retaliate or seem to mind, it was thought that 'they rather liked it'. If the boys followed this up by whistling at the girls during the show, the attendant came round and ushered them out. In regard to general rowdyism, one of the boys said that everyone behaved quietly unless 'a few ruffians' got in.

The children, on their best behaviour before the Committee, were rather reticient about their preferences in the way of films, but one of the boys, pressed very hard for a verdict on instructional nature films, admitted that they 'could be a bit trying'. Love-stories were 'rather trying' too, so perhaps Mr Legge was worrying rather too much about the policeman and the cook. Perhaps, too, the policeman and the cook were decorous compared with all they could learn of life in their own over-crowded homes. Said Mr John Massey, Court Missionary and Probation Officer of the Old Street Police Court:

> Just imagine what the cinemas mean to tens of thousands of poor children herded together in one room . . . six or eight families under the same roof. For a few hours at the picture house at the corner they can find a breathing space, warmth, music (the more music the better), and the pictures, where they can have a real laugh, a cheer and sometimes a shout. . . . Those who have the least knowledge of the habits, the difficulties and the squalid lives of these one and two-roomed tenants talk the most foolish things against the cinema. . . . What is needed today is real, first-hand knowledge of the conditions in which the poor live.

Another sympathetic and knowledgeable champion of the picture palace—and a particularly valuable one, because he had done his research very thoroughly and circulated his findings to colleagues in other parts of the country for their comments—was the Chief Constable of Edinburgh, Mr Roderick Ross, MVO. He stated emphatically that the social change which coincided with the opening of the first picture palaces was an immediate reduction of drunkenness. The admitted recent increase in 'juvenile delinquency' (as we have now ceased to call it) coincided, not with the opening of the first picture palace, but with the departure of the fathers from their homes four years later on the outbreak of war. Mr Barnett, Court Missioner of the Westminster Police Court, added that the same thing happened on the outbreak of the South African War, and that there were no picture palaces then. The Chief Constables of Dundee and Aberdeen also said that drunkenness had decreased; and the Chief Constable of Beverley gave the picture houses the credit for the fact that cases of drunkenness among the thousands of troops in camp were only one in every thousand men.

The Chief Constable of Edinburgh, who clearly knew and loved his fellow citizens, went on to give a rather touching picture of the city's young women without their men:

It is the custom in picture houses in the poorer quarters of the city for a considerable number of women with children in arms to attend late at night. In one picture house in one evening after 8 p.m. no less than forty-two women with children in arms were seen to leave the premises. This is a matter to be deplored, but it is no doubt due to the fact that most of the husbands of these women are at present on active service with His Majesty's forces, and no doubt the women are glad to have a little relaxation from the weary round which is theirs; and being unable, of course, to leave the children behind have perforce to take them with them.

This happened up and down the country, but not everyone was as understanding as the Chief Constable of Edinburgh; the Medical Officer of Health for Torquay, a year earlier, had asked for the co-operation of licence holders in stamping out the practice. However, perhaps a year of mounting casualty lists may have changed his point of view.

But to return to Mr Ross, giving evidence before the Public Morality Council. He went on to say that any allegedly indecent films of which he had heard had proved not to be indecent enough for police action, but that he deplored the showing of suggestive films because of the suggestibility of young people. He added that he did not know of any case of children actually imitating crimes they had seen on the screen, but he thought that displays of the activities of criminals were dangerous, because boys needed an outlet for their love of adventure.

Various Chief Constables who, in the main, agreed with the Chief Constable of Edinburgh, could not go all the way with him about imitable crime: Bootle and Brighton both said that some stealing seemed to have been inspired by tricks seen on the films, and Huddersfield and Rotherham had both had outbreaks of theft by boys calling themselves the 'Clutching Hand Gang' after the showing in local cinemas of a film about a gang of that name.

Evidence that cinema-going causes children to steal who would not otherwise have done so is very scarce: the cinema habit may, in this respect, be comparable to hypnosis, which is supposed not to be able to make a person go completely counter to his true nature. But *fashions* in crime, like fashions in speech, singing or ways of doing one's hair, these, it does seem, are another matter. Indeed, I do not see how anyone could argue differently, who has watched the superficial Americanization of society in this country in the twenties and thirties of this century and reflected that in those days the great majority of British people had never met an American anywhere except on the cinema screen.

As for the Chief Constable of Brechin, he condemned the whole new entertainment out of hand: he said that it would probably die a natural death in a few years, and a good thing too, as then perhaps the country people would go to church again (at present they were not doing so and a number of chapels had been turned into picture houses).

The Chief Constable of Guildford said that cinemas were full of germs. Moreover, the darkness was the cause of many abuses, 'and one in particular where young men and young women attend together, not for the purpose of following the pictures, but, owing to the darkness, to become spoony, and to work up passions which may be described as "initiative immorality". Cases have been reported to me of young women who have fallen through having been overcome in the way related.'

Mr Cecil Leeson, Secretary of the Howard Association, had something to tell the Committee about the plight of the child who was not really wanted anywhere for the hour or two immediately after school:

> He leaves school at four, often earlier. If he goes home, neither father nor mother are there. An elder sister prepares his tea, or maybe a neighbour gives him some, but no one really wants him. He requires to be interested, and positively the only interesting things still remaining in his little world are the picture palace and the street it stands in. Left thus to themselves, the wonder is that children should stick at anything to get away from their dullness. Bundles of energy, suppressed during the few hours' confinement at school, now in reaction, spoiling for something to vent themselves upon, and with no one to say them nay—that is the condition of these lads. Some of them steal. The wonder is that so few of them do. For there is risk to stealing, and excitement, which is what healthy-minded lads need, and which, if it avoid the ultra-sensational, is good for them. When the charge that lads are taught to steal

by the films comes to be properly investigated, it will probably be found . . . that the great majority of them steal because they are dull.

We are much indebted to the cheap cinemas of the days before television for having given children something safe and lawful to do in that uncomfortable gap between school and the evening reunion of the whole family. It is a time of day which even the most dedicated teachers and youth club workers hope to have to themselves, to have a rest and a quiet cup of tea and recoup their energies before a new spurt of activity in the evening, and when mothers who have gladly given up their jobs for babies and little children are beginning to think, of their older school-age sons and daughters, 'Surely to goodness *now* they can amuse themselves for a little while without getting into mischief?' I had not realized that the latch-key kids were with us quite so early in history, but they have certainly been a feature of the social scene ever since, and before they could switch on 'the Telly' the prospect for town children was dull in the extreme.

My favourite witness is Mrs Basil Henriques, a compassionate woman with a flair for understanding what were not then called teen-agers. In the ordinary way, she ran a girls' club at St George's-in-the-East and her husband ran the boys' club round the corner. But now he had gone to the wars, so she ran both. Other witnesses and members of the committee had agreed that when a young person reached puberty, or the school-leaving age of fourteen, he or she ceased to be a child. Mrs Henriques would have none of this.

> Most of the *children* [she said firmly] are tailors or cigarette-makers, and the work is not a great strain on them mentally, so they have plenty of time to think and talk of things, and in the evening when they have finished their work they feel they must have some excitement. Now the housing question settles the matter, because down there nine or ten people are living in one house, and the luxury of only four people to one bedroom is something to be envied. You will thus see that it is impossible for the children to stop indoors in most cases. The houses are usually rather dirty, and in many cases there is a consumptive father and the smaller children are screaming.

In Time of War

Anyway, there is every inducement for the children to go into the streets. Round about St George's there are quite a lot of undesirable houses and loose women, and the amount of evil which surrounds the children is appalling. It is either a question of stopping in the streets and seeing what is going on, or going to the pictures; and there are a number of cases where the parents like them to go to the pictures because of these things. The next point is that it is a dark place, and if you have a young lady it is very convenient to go there. It is also a convenient rendezvous for family parties, but the elder children do not go with their parents: they go with their 'bird'. The expression down there is that you take your 'bird' to the pictures.

Here, as nearly always in the annals of the 1917 meeting, 'the children' turns out to mean 'the boys'. The 'birds' in the foregoing paragraph are only mentioned as adjuncts to the boys, and indeed, as a rule it was with the effect of the cinema on boys that the pressure groups and the Press were most concerned. There was a curious ambivalence in the attitude towards the girls, when they were mentioned at all. It seems to have been assumed that they were too sensible to put their future at risk by stealing, but abysmally silly when it came to believing that luxury on the scale of the Hollywood film-stars was within the reach of every shopgirl in London.

Soon after writing these lines, I had the pleasure of meeting Mrs (later Lady) Henriques. She was very old and, as it turned out, that day was her last birthday, but she was still working in her office among her friends and neighbours, a stone's throw from Aldgate East underground station, and still keeping the fortitude and the sense of humour that had sustained her through two world wars, an uneasy peace and the loss of her beloved husband. She told me that at the 1917 inquiry the phalanx of clergymen on the opposite side of the table kept their eyes shut. She wondered whether they were asleep or just trying to visualize the dreadful things of which they had been hearing. I expressed my admiration of the way in which she had carried on, only married a year, with her husband in danger, and with a double burden on her shoulders, and she looked almost shocked that I should think this worthy of comment: 'It was one's duty'.

Lest anyone should think that the 1917 gathering was only concerned with the moral safety of the children of the poor and that the children of the rich had been given *carte blanche* to go to the devil in their own way, it is interesting to record that, while the Headmaster of Harrow thought that cinema-going was, on the whole, quite a harmless amusement, the Headmaster of Eton would have liked to see all children excluded from the picture palaces up to the age of eighteen!

Finally, lest anyone should think that everyone present was wrapped in a philistine oblivion of the artistic possibilities of the new entertainment, and that no one had a particularly impressive command of the English language, let the veteran film-manufacturer Cecil Hepworth have the last word:

> Cranks and faddists from time immemorial have arisen to condemn every art for the sake of the grain of evil of which they can see it to be capable. It is for us to see that this great new art, fraught with wonderful possibilities of enlightenment for us and our children and our children's children and for our nation as a whole, shall not be emasculated, shall not be rendered harmless and therefore powerless for good as well.

Reluctantly, I leave the committee-room of the National Council of Public Morals. There is much warmth and humanity here, and when—as often happens—they sound very funny to us today, well, the human race *is* very funny and we forget it at our peril. It does no harm to remember that some of our own most cherished certainties will probably sound just as ridiculous sixty years on.

In consequence of the inquiry the Council concluded that there ought to be a State censorship of cinematograph films, and more light in cinemas. Despite short-lived attempts here and there to achieve 'morality lighting'—a gentle pink or amber glow in the auditorium during the showing of the films—before long there was on average *less* light in cinemas, as in 1917 it was still customary to put the house lights up at the end of each reel of film while the next reel was put on the projector, and this break in continuity soon ceased. As for censorship, at the time of writing its complete abolition seems much more likely than the introduction of a state system, but one never knows. Anyway, if such a thing should come about, it could not be attributed to the deliberations of these anxious and good-hearted people, most of them long since dead. The Committee of Inquiry had run true to form.

After the useful letting off of steam in the 1917 inquiry, the guardians seem, for the time being, to have been almost reconciled to the motion pictures, not least because Lord Beaverbrook, the Minister of Information, had found that the best way of drumming necessary information into the heads of the populace was to get at them, as the travelling showmen had long been doing, by means of travelling cinema vans. The cinema trade resented the competition. It was rebuked for saying so, but the Government took note of the complaint and promised to restrict its shows, in populated districts where there were commercial cinemas, to one night at a time.

Military tribunals became a little less grudging in their attitude to the deferment of call-up of cinema staffs. The trade hoped that this might be partly because of a new consciousness of their usefulness to the community: an article in the issue of *Kine Weekly* of 21 March 1918 says prophetically, '. . . one can only conceive a Government closing down the kinemas in the most extreme urgency, and then with considerable danger of antagonising a public opinion which the motion picture entertainment does much to keep healthy'.

But the trade still had its troubles: it must not be supposed that the cinemas had embarked on a period of unprecedented peace and joy. They may have kept public opinion healthy, but the terrible influenza epidemic of 1918-19 was about to begin, and cinemas were blamed as one of the chief centres for disseminating germs. Many local authorities forbade the attendance of children under fifteen. The Paisley magistrates were still taking this action as late as March 1919. *Kine Weekly* pointed out crossly that 'the attendants had not been stricken at Paisley Picture Theatre', and asked, 'Has not the time arrived—is it not almost past?—for the kinematograph industry to clear itself of the slander that kinemas are a source of spreading infection?'

There were troubles within the industry too. In March 1918, cinema and theatre managers in Aberdeen were having some bother over the demand of the Theatrical Employees' Association for a 50 per cent increase in wages. Well, bearing in mind that key members of cinema staffs were only receiving from £2 to £3 a week, a 50 per cent pay rise was not going to turn them into bloated cigar-smoking capitalists overnight. But all the same, it was an electrifying demand for those days, and it says much for the skill of trained projectionists and not a little for the fundamental fair-mindedness of the trade that *Kine Weekly* continued to give credit where credit was due. It seems that, in spite of their generosity to 'the decorative sex' when there seemed no prospect of the war ever ending, the managers had now discovered how well off they were with experienced labour in times of peace, and would not be sorry to usher women out of 'the box' for good, or at any rate for a great many years. 'The importance of the operator and of the operator's qualifications', says *Kine Weekly*, 'has been learned in grief and bad language by innumerable managements. . . . The operator is one of the most important individuals on the exhibiting side of the industry, and the only alternative to his adequate recognition appears to be a general increase of time rates to compensate for the ever-dwindling life of the film'.

In short, the trade must close its ranks. Now that there was hope of the common enemy, the Germans, being routed before too long, the traditional adversaries, the Government and the local authorities, must be confronted once again. In March 1918, with the terrible spring offensive in progress, it would have been unbecoming to make a fuss about the early closing of cinemas to save fuel, and this the proprietors did not do; the central Government had their whole-hearted support. But the brief sense of community of interests was drawing to a close and did not outlast the war. By March 1919, cinema operators who, on joining up as electricians, had been classified as 'Group 26', had now turned into cinema operators again for purposes of demobilization and were classified as 'Group 41', well back in the queue. One of them, still in France, complained, 'the Kinema Trade seems to be regarded as of no importance by the Army and Air authorities, and I think we are being treated badly by them after the good work we have done in supplying amusements to the troops, both on active service and at home'.

As to the local authorities, they did get an incidental pat on the back: we learn that in March 1919, despite the very serious housing shortage, proposals were still being made to demolish houses to make room for more kinemas. 'The folly of such suggestions,' says *Kine Weekly*, 'is sufficiently apparent':

Throughout the war the Trade assisted the authorities in every possible way in its power, and naturally looks for some consideration now that the crucial period has passed. Whether it is likely to receive any is a matter for conjecture, but no useful purpose can be served by alienating sympathy and arousing official opposition by any such utter disregard for the general welfare as proposals to destroy houses for the purpose of creating kinema sites involve. We are glad to see that in the cases in which the matter has so far arisen the local authorities are holding over licences and refusing to make ejection orders.

But soon we are in the heart of the Sunday opening quarrel which broke out sporadically over the country for many years and did much to embitter relations between the trade and various local licensing authorities. At the moment, Middlesex was in the forefront of the battle, and it was now that poor Mr Goodwin, Chairman of the London and Home Counties Cinematograph Exhibitors' Association—who, it may be remembered, had blotted his copybook already at the Public Morality Council's inquiry by approving of couples sitting in cinemas with their arms round each other's waists—learned from his opponents' posters on putting up for election to the Council that 'a vote for Goodwin was a vote against God'.

Over the industrial north of the country, the pattern of the uneasy peace which separated the two world wars was already beginning to take shape in shadows more ominous than squabbles about the proper observance of the Sabbath—shadows as yet hardly noticed, for there is only a little news item, in April 1919, on an inside page of *Kine Weekly*, about the reason why the people of Blackburn can still afford to go to the picture house.

> Though there is a good deal of unemployment in Blackburn owing to slackness in the cotton trade, the kinemas are doing well. Their success is likely to continue as long as the unemployment benefit goes on. The latter has been a boon to the kinemas, for without it there would have been little money in circulation.

And in Barrow the situation was the same.

There could be no more eloquent testimony to what the cinemas meant to the poorest people of this country in the years between the wars. And if anyone, today, is still found to ask, as many did ask in those days, whether the unemployed really needed to go to the pictures, one can only give the answer King Lear gave to his heartless daughter:

> Allow not nature more than nature needs,
> Man's life is cheap as beast's . . .

The cinemas visit was not only good value for money, it was an emblem, a flag kept flying in token of no surrender and an unconquerable hope of better things to come.

3
The Restless Twenties

Stars came thick and fast, from the beginning of the reign of Clara Bow to the arrival of Al Jolson and the talkies. Ronald Colman began his Hollywood career in 1922, Gary Cooper and Greta Garbo in 1926, the year of the death of Rudolph Valentino. Later came the screen début of the Marx Brothers, Frederic March and Mickey Mouse. Among the other favourites were Chaplin, John Gilbert, the Barrymores, Douglas Fairbanks, Harold Lloyd, Buster Keaton, Ramon Novarro.

Some films to remember: *The Four Horsemen of the Apocalypse, Nanook of the North, The Covered Wagon, The Iron Horse, Robin Hood, The Thief of Bagdad, The Gold Rush, The Ten Commandments, The Battleship Potemkin, The Big Parade, The Freshman, The Eagle, Son of the Sheik, The General, Mother, The Jazz Singer, The Singing Fool, King of Kings, Atlantic, Blackmail, The Blue Angel, Drifters, The Fall of the House of Usher.*

3
The Restless Twenties

When at last all the young men who were coming home from the war had duly arrived, it became apparent that, while some had had enough fighting to last them the rest of their lives, others had not, especially when they had been drinking. In Dundee it was found that the social customs of cinema-going and getting drunk were by no means mutually exclusive. One exhibitor, who had fourteen attendants to about a thousand patrons, needed them all in times of stress. One night, he needed more—or so a member of his family thought, rushing helpfully into the fray. The police arrived and arrested a fair haul of trouble-makers. They telephoned afterwards from the station to say 'There's a young man here who *says* he's your son'. Whether this experience had a daunting effect upon the young man, I do not know. But the fact remains that when at last a successor to the proprietor of this cinema was needed, the mantle fell, not upon him but on his sister.

But for the moment, the father of the family was still firmly in command; and now, just after the war and towards the end of his reign, it is appropriate to say a little more about this remarkable man, as good a representative as one could find of the best kind of independent exhibitor of the first decade of real, purpose-built cinemas, the beginning of that brief era when, for cinema proprietors, independence was the order of the day.

The people of Dundee needed the manager of the family picture house. Before his arrival on the scene, they saw their pictures in a tent. The owners of the tent knew what they were about, for they had run a fairground picture booth before settling down in Dundee. That had been better than nothing, but not warm, dry or safe enough to make the long, hard winter much happier for the poorer people of the city, and certainly not, for the men, a serious rival to the public house.

This exhibitor and his partner, teetotallers both, went into the film world almost as much because they hated drunkenness as because they loved films, and we have the testimony of the Chief Constable of their city that their campaign against drink met with some success. Another thing they hated was dirt; they had the cinema scrubbed out every day. Like all good Scotsmen, they had a proper regard for education, of which, they believed, the working man needed more, if he were to take his due share in the counsels of the nation (a share which, as staunch members of the Independent Labour Party, they did not undervalue); so they took care to include documentary films in their programmes at a time when such items were by no means general. Finally, they loved children. They were pioneers of children's shows long before these were a common feature of the cinema scene. There was always a special programme for the afternoon show, at a time when the general idea was that, as long as the film was not outrageously unsuitable, one need not bother what one shovelled up to the juvenile customers, because they would take anything. The cost of admission was a penny, and each child was given a farthing bar of Fry's chocolate, which the proprietor insisted must be wrapped in silver paper. This sort of service is not a recipe for getting rich quick. It deserves to be remembered.

If this proprietor should now be accused of paternalism, he would probably agree, and be surprised to learn that, in the philosophy of today, he was being offered a deadly insult. He might well be surprised. There is a good deal of evidence that children and young people need fatherly care and concern from someone, whether they want it or not, and there were some thousands of children in Britain then who had no fathers of their own.

This manager became ill in 1922. Luckily for the family business, and for the neighbourhood, his daughter, though still little more than a schoolgirl, was already well grounded in the management of a picture house and ready to take over. The Bailies of Dundee looked benevolently but cautiously upon this new recruit, so young, and a woman in what was now once again a man's world, before anyone had invented the expression 'Women's Lib'. The other managers, she said, might take a chance now and then in little things, but she never could. Her mother had to sign all the contracts, a task which she shouldered reluctantly, as in addition to a dislike of signing things, she had no love for the cinema. She was still not allowing her little daughter to 'go to the pictures' when father said one day, 'Hurry up and finish your tea, I want you to take the pay-box.' 'I had no idea,' she remembers, 'what the pay-box was, or where I was to take it, till I found myself sitting at the receipt of custom. It took me the whole of the first house to cash up ready for the second. Yes . . . I learned all the jobs around the picture house the hard way, by doing them myself. Cashier, stand-in usherette, assistant in the rewind-room, runner between cinemas with reels of film—I did it all from time to time.'

Yes, she did it all from time to time. And she ran the picture house till 1959 and became the only woman representative on the Central Council of the Cinematograph Exhibitors' Association, which body she also represented on the Advisory Sub-Committee of the Cinema Consultative Committee.

As she will be with us for the rest of my story, I shall have more to say about her cinema later on. In the meantime I will just add that, though this family was an outstanding example, there were a good many proprietors and managers up and down the country who carried on the same tradition of imaginative service to the people among whom they lived. It is not surprising that the poorer people of Britian were as loyal as ever to their neighbourhood picture-house, and that the villagers and inhabitants of very small towns, who had not had one before, were happy to realize their dream, as soon as 'luxury building' was once more allowed. Not all the luxury building was particularly luxurious, but that did not matter: the patrons loved their 'local' in a way which has been vividly described to me by Sydney Barnes, a founder member of the audience of my own first 'local', the Scala, built at New Milton in Hampshire in 1920. As a schoolboy, he queued every

Friday evening from 6.30 to 7 with his young friends, waiting to cheer the arrival of the films by motor van when, sometimes only minutes before the advertized starting time, along came Felix the Cat, and the Pathé News, and the 'big picture'—and the pianist, later to be supplanted by a radiogram. The picture was projected from behind the screen, which I believe was very rare, though Herbert Wilcox in his book *Twenty-five Thousand Sunsets* does tell of one 'rough industrial hall' in Yorkshire at this time where the screen was hung half-way along the long tunnel-like auditorium and the least wealthy patrons (all children) sat behind it with their backs to it, viewing the picture through pieces of looking-glass so as to get the captions the right way round. At the Scala, it was not unknown for the captions to appear the wrong way round, which added to the general hilarity. The Scala was a timber building, with a flat floor, except for the three back rows of seats which were raised above the others and were padded, and so of course cost more. The commissionaire was a magnificent figure in his gold-braided uniform: they often called him Rudolph Valentino. There was a chucker-out, too, a man of imposing presence whose very appearance was enough to bring about a perfect calm.

In time, Sydney Barnes left school and was privileged to be employed as office boy at an estate agent's under the very same roof as his beloved Scala Cinema. On wet mornings, after sweeping out the office, he was allowed to take the rubbish through the cinema to the dustbins at the back. In this way he said, 'I was lucky enough to find pieces of films which had been shown on the previous evening. I still have some of those pieces . . . one is of Monty Banks trying to pull up his umbrella (open) from a street drain-grid'. Mr Barnes nobly lent me his cherished bits of film so that I could see them for myself: one of them was a little caption from the news, 'England and Wales draw at Twickenham 11 each'.

In due time, Mr Barnes did his courting at his local cinema, like some thousands of his fellow countrymen in those far-off days, and by the time the grand Waverley Cinema arrived in 1929 to put the Scala's nose out of joint, he was engaged. Sydney and Susie were among the twenty or so patrons who could not bear to say good-bye to the Scala before they must, and were loyally occupying their usual seats even on the new palace's opening night.

Another regular patron of the Scala was a homesick little girl of fourteen (now Mrs C. M. House and a grandmother), who had come up from the West Country to earn her living and sent home to her mother a picture postcard of 'the picture house where I always go'. She showed me the postcard, still a cherished family memento of old times.

It is of this time, too, that my friend Rosemary is talking in her vivid description of a little picture-house in Thirsk, 'where the manager always stood in front of the screen and before any dramatic moment kept calling out "*Quiet* please!" to a really very docile audience—but he might have intended his words for the pianist, who played, I imagine extempore, to what she thought was on the screen, but generally she failed to keep up with the action, so we had thundering horses' hooves in the middle of the clinch or close-up.'

Those of us, and there were many, even in the better-off sections of the population and in the swinging twenties, who still did not in our wildest dreams imagine having a motor-car and rushing about madly in search of diversion, and who lived far away from the nearest large town, could not afford to be over-sophisticated in our choice of pleasures, and the old pattern of cinema-going was good enough for us. And it was good enough for children everywhere, however intelligent they were, however varied their other interests. Malcolm was a hard-up, clever London boy whose parents intended him to mind his book and further his education by winning scholarships, as indeed he duly did. But he went to 'the pictures' as often as funds would allow, and on several different intellectual levels: with his mates for the fun of running with the pack and yelling 'Bang! Bang!' in the Westerns and *Shoulder Arms!*; with his family, including his mother, to *Intolerance* ('We were very sedate, and she was much moved'); with his friends again, for the thrill of the picture, to *The Four Horsemen of the Apocalypse* ('We were spellbound').

But the older and more wordly-wise patrons in the big towns and cities were becoming rather more selective. *The Times* was restless. It had said, as early as March 1919, that change was in the air, adding that 'even the humours of Mr Charles Chaplin can grow wearisome after a time' (and this a year before Mr Charles Chaplin revisited his native land and was greeted with transports of delight).

The Times had at last concluded that the cinematograph theatre was not a passing craze but had come to stay, and what was more, it was not merely for children, or for grown-ups with an hour to waste between trains: 'The extraordinary success of such places as the New Gallery Cinema, the West End Cinema, the Marble Arch Pavilion, and the London Opera House . . . has proved that if the programme is sufficiently attractive the same audience will go to the picture-theatre week in and week out throughout the year.'

But in one way, *The Times* added, the cinematograph had not changed: it 'is essentially a family entertainment and the programme must be above suspicion. There will be no room in the theatre of the future for the film which "skates on thin ice". . . .' Films of adventure, it thinks, fill the bill very well and 'a film like that based on the American novel *Tarzan of the Apes*, which is about to be shown in this country, will be welcome in any programme'.

The Times thought that while we in this country could not hope to make another *Tarzan of the Apes*, there were plenty of opportunities, which 'the English manufacturer' should hasten to seize, of making the steady stream of family entertainment which would be needed now for ever.

In fact, it was not so easy. British film-making had virtually dried up during the war. There were other uses for men; and there were other uses for the ingredients of nitrate film stock. Which is one reason why, despite the later efforts of the British Film Institute to preserve the records of the past, much of the pre-1918 film scene has perished as though it had never been. Now that film-making was again possible in Britain, the industry had to start from scratch, handicapped by the fact that many British cinemas were committed to the 'block-booking', sight unseen, of packages of miscellaneous American films, the bad and indifferent no less than the good. There were few signs, as yet, that the public minded this state of affairs, for many of them were still happy to go to the pictures to see almost anything and be gregarious and keep warm, while the more sophisticated audiences in the centre of big cities got the best films sooner and more often in their 'first run' houses than did the under-privileged 'out in the sticks'. Also, there was an engaging gusto about even the indifferent American product which the British could not hope to match simply by saying to themselves that it would be economically satisfactory if they made a lot of films and conquered a fairer share of the home market. Where art is concerned—and even in what concerns that curious hybrid the 'movie', part art, part commerce—there is no substitute for the whole-hearted urge to create something, however silly. In terms of sheer vigour and vitality, one may get less out of creative work than the creators put into it, but one is most unlikely to get more.

What was congenial to the British, as soon as they once more had the money and the labour, was building more and more splendid cinemas and beautifying the old ones. In this line, it cannot be said that they were innovators, and their conservatism was a source of dissatisfaction to many sophisticated people. But it is very doubtful whether the movie-going millions wanted innovation. More probably, they wanted something rich rather than strange—luxuries of a palatial kind that had been on the fringes of their consciousness before, but always out of reach. If, as was soon all too sadly clear, we could not make a world fit for heroes to live in, a substitute Valhalla for an occasional festive afternoon or evening out was better than nothing, especially if, besides seeing a picture, you could dance and feast in the same marble halls.

Mr Sol Levy was among those quickest off the mark, with the help of the exuberant fancy of Mr Val Prince, who, having just decorated the Futurist Cinema in Birmingham which had had to wait for the end of the war, now turned his fertile inventiveness to giving a new look to the Broadway Palladium at Ealing, the Kilburn Grange Picture House, the Maida Vale Picture House and the Coronet Theatre, Notting Hill, all of them within easy reach of patrons whose own homes were nothing like palaces. Thirsting for the glamour and colour which the war years had put even farther out of reach than usual, the patrons luxuriated in ballrooms gay with mermaids and goldfish and butterflies, in Jacobean restaurants full of pennants and shields and coat-armour, in tea-rooms lit by drum-shaped lanterns suspended from Chinese dragons, or treated throughout 'in the Egyptian style'. *The Times* considered it was all very tasteful. I was not there myself, not yet having emerged from my cool, sequestered country way of life, and being busy with my education; but judging by the bindings of some books I bought with prize money only a few years later, I am sure I would have been enraptured.

The new picture-theatres came thick and fast in the next few years, and increasingly the most fashionable of the halls built for other purposes went over to films for part or all of the time. The Empire, the Alhambra, the Palace, the London Pavilion, all found that variety, or even straight plays, no longer sufficed to fill the bill. The London Opera House became the Stoll Picture Theatre and started to make money for the first time—without severing its ancient links with music, for Dr Tootell and his recitals on the newly installed Jardine pipe organ soon became rival attractions to 'Mr Chaplin and Mr Fairbanks'. The Stoll soon added feasting and listening to lectures to its other attractions, and even included a club for picture-goers, at which leading producers and directors (for so, by now, the 'manufacturers' were called) expounded their art, and 'stars' appeared from time to time. In general 'cultural awareness' the Stoll almost rivalled the old-established New Gallery, the doyen of the fashionable purpose-built picture theatres, which from the first had hoped to keep open house for every sort of intellectual pursuit.

The richest of the new cinemas were opulent indeed. The Regent at Brighton was a perfectly splendid place: it not only cost £400,000, which is a very satisfying thought, it had what was believed to be the largest theatre balcony in the country, and size is satisfying too, as long as you can get enough people to fill your building, though it becomes something of an embarrassment in times of recession. It was built in the shape of 'Dr Horton's church at Hampstead', the fan with the point chopped off, which further experience had confirmed as the best shape for cinemas. The auditorium was decorated with allegorical pictures of Carnival and hung with antique white marble candelabra. There was a café like the wardroom of an eighteenth-century three-decker, and an Italian Renaissance restaurant; and if all that was not enough for you, surely, with a roof-garden as well, your cup of joy would be full. The Liverpool Stoll was to have a roof-garden too, and an Italian Renaissance façade with imposing columns surmounted by a dome (the Italian Renaissance influence was very strong just now).

Those who were of a more prosaic turn of mind, more prone to concentrate on such advantages as the best air-conditioning system in the country, could go north to Glasgow, to the Picture House in Sauchiehall Street, for five million cubic feet of fresh air every hour, complete filtering, cleaning, and heating or cooling as necessary, every three minutes, and ozone galore in tanks near

The proprietor of a family picture house, with his family and staff, 1924

A town picture house – the Princess Theatre, Dundee, 1926

The projection room of the Tower Annexe, Peckham, circa 1923

the roof. Not that the Glasgow Picture House was without its share of beauty and luxury: it had a splendid fountain playing in the foyer and a truly magnificent fireplace. If music was your special joy, the Futurist, Birmingham, like the London Stoll, set special store by it: it had piped music in the café, as well as musical interludes on two afternoons a week. By the middle of the twenties there was a positive explosion of cinema building, and the cinemas themselves were becoming more overblown, answering a deeply felt need for some contrast to the slough of depression which the country was just entering. Cultivated taste deplored the ebullience of cinema decoration as it was developing by 1928: *The Times*, which had praised the Regal Cinema at Brighton and the Shepherd's Bush Pavilion which, as late as 1924, won an award from the Royal Institute of British Architects, was scathing about the interior decorations of the Empire, Leicester Square, opened in 1928. They 'are overwhelming, leading to the inescapable conclusion that the film will not stand on its own merits and that the public must be dazed into submission'. Nor did it like the interior, or the 'fruity capitals', of the new Regal at Marble Arch. '... there is a limit to the amount of ornamental expression that any form of entertainment will bear in architecture—unless the aim is merely to advertise money to burn. The additional suggestion of the newer houses is that the film has failed and must be buried under mountains of marble, plate-glass and gilding...'

This is not how it seemed to the average patron, enjoying one of his hard-earned evenings out in the West End. If there were indeed a suggestion of money to burn, he liked the suggestion, remote as it was from the cares of daily life. He would have appreciated the gusto of the publicity booklet compiled later by Metro-Goldwyn-Mayer themselves, with its insistence on just those features that *The Times* deplored:

> The Empire was then without doubt the last word in palatial opulence. With its gilded dome, sweeping staircase, huge foyer, elaborate chandeliers, the hand-made carpet for the entrance hall and foyer (it measured 43 feet wide, 100 feet long, weighed a ton, took six months to make and needed 20 men to lift it with difficulty), the three coloured velvet pelmets, marbles, gleaming wood, mirrors and superbly

decorated ceiling it offered just that luxury touch that helps to make a night out.

Yes, I well remember that carpet. It was a thing to wonder at. You felt as if you were sinking into it up to the ankles. Many of us thought, before, during and after the Second World War, that, just for a change, exuberance could not go too far.

For a panoramic view of the cinemas of the first half of the century and later, the reader cannot do better than consult Dennis Sharp's copiously illustrated book *The Picture Palace and Other Buildings for the Movies* (Hugh Evelyn, 1969). Here, we have only time for a fleeting glance at the surroundings in which the people managed to enjoy themselves despite present hardship and the gathering shadows of impending disaster.

For in the vexed and restless twenties virtually everyone was going to the pictures—looking for luxury, looking for a window on the new world of sex and violence which was believed to lie beyond the western horizon; looking for freedom, for a new art and a new culture, or for somewhere to be close in darkness to his or her love; or, at a very young age, just for somewhere to go for the exhilaration of an evening outside the home, and for the thrills of the moving image. And if what the moving image conveyed to your childish mind was forbidden, well, so much the better. 'Virtually everyone,' of course, included many members of that nebulous and shifting entity 'the Establishment', and these people experienced a good deal of secret exhilaration and enjoyment themselves, as well indeed they might. The films included an unconscionable deal of nonsense and unworthy trash: how should it be otherwise, with the ever-open doors of the thousands of picture palaces needing to be fed, week after week, year after year, with a steady stream of patrons—in default of which constant patronage the whole huge edifice of motion picture entertainment would fall crashing to the ground? When thousands of films are needed, some of them are bound to be bad. But most people could find something to satisfy them in the rich variety that this decade showered upon them: in Chaplin or Fairbanks, Garbo or Pola Negri or Valentino, Laughton or Lloyd, Keaton or the Barrymores or Dietrich or Dracula or Mickey Mouse; in the pictures as various as *Greed, The Iron Horse, Nanook of the North, The Big Parade, Ben Hur*—which seemed likely to run for ever in the West End—or the more dubious but equally powerful artistic blandishments of Cecil B. de Mille—not to mention, at the end of the decade, the first uncertain accents of the 'talkies' bursting cacophonously upon the astonished world.

It must not be thought, however, that everyone was pleased. Far from it. The deep-rooted puritan conviction that one ought not to be pleased with that which is intended to give pleasure was still strong in the British people. And indeed, it was all too easy to pick holes in the films, if one were given to xenophobia, or anxiously concerned for the welfare of children or of what they still, in unguarded moments, called the lower orders, or just intolerant of 'false values', bad history and bad art. *The Times* was all these things. Almost the last time that it permitted itself to relax, as it might if it so far forgot its dignity as to ride on the merry-go-round at the fair, was at a children's matinée in a London suburb in May 1920.

> The average film, of course, is admirably suited to the intellect of a child, and all that has to be done is to reduce the price of admission to the level of a child's pocket. The process is wonderfully simple. The price of admission is reduced from 6d to 3d and one has what is triumphantly described as a Children's Matinée. The fact remains, however, that although it is unpretentious, a children's matinée is a remarkable experience. Thoroughly to enjoy it the intruding grown-up must put on the simple faith of a child. He must be childlike and bland, and above all he must forget to be superior. If he will try to forget for a few hours any theories on the film and crime, or the film and education, and just be content to think of the film as an afternoon's diversion, he may enter into the company of the elect, who regard a film, a dog-fight, a Punch and Judy show, as created for one purpose only—that of their own private and personal entertainment. If he fails to enjoy the experience he must either be very clever or very foolish. He will almost certainly regret that the cinematograph was not invented when he, too was young enough to live in Arcadia.

The writer went on to recreate the unforgettable atmosphere of a large gathering of small children, which does not seem to have altered much in the intervening fifty years.

The ground floor of the hall was thick with esctatic and squirming children. They squirmed not only with their bodies but with their tongues, and the result resembled the remarks of the chorus in the *Frogs* of Aristophanes. The clamour was amazing even before the lights went down, and when the title of the film flickered uncertainly onto the screen the noise changed to a roar of the kind that is usually associated with an 'infuriated mob'.

There was nothing wrong, by the lights of 1920, with the entertainment which followed, a story about the defeat by the forces of law and order of a wicked mandarin. The children's matinée seldom contained anything which even that more cautious age considered too sexy, violent or frightening for the very young. But such shows were then rare; nobody could call them educational; and worse, they did not stop children from going to the ordinary cinema shows as often as they could, and this was very often indeed. The whole embattled forces of the teachers, the local authorities and miscellaneous pressure groups were hardly a match for a resourceful and resolute child. And if to be increasingly concerned with sex and crime and violence is to grow up, then the films were certainly growing up, and undoubtedly many of them were becoming less suitable for children. In consequence, as early as 1923 the London County Council attached a condition to its cinema licences that unaccompanied children under the age of sixteen were not to be admitted to the cinema when A films were being shown. And gradually, overcoming their deep-rooted dislike of meekly following in London's wake or, worse still, doing what the Home Office recommended, the greater number of the other local authorities in England and Wales followed suit; some, later in the decade, even tried to exclude children from A films altogether. (In Scotland the A certificate was always advisory only.)

But this was not the end of the matter. Deliberate flouting of the condition led to prosecution and was rare. But it was easy to evade the intention of the new rule, which was of course that a child should be accompanied by his own parent or guardian or by someone deputizing for him. No manager could ask for documentary evidence of the relationship of some of the ill-assorted couples who appeared at the box-office window, and the cinema queues, which were a permanent feature of the evening street scene in those days, were besieged by little boys importuning the grown-ups, 'Will you take me in, please Mister?'. 'Mister' very often thought the regulation pointless. After all, he had been reared in a rough, tough school of go-as-you-please entertainment, and in the last ten years he had seen worse things than the most horrible film was likely to contain. He readily obliged.

And even when the rule was obeyed, the standards of classification of films into the A and U categories by the British Board of Film Censors were usually under attack somewhere in the country. The cinematograph industry attracted researchers and investigators as a plum-tree brings out the wasps in a hot August. But it did not, till much later, produce swarms of experts and specialists in the 'sociology of film', and child psychology was still an infant art; so film censorship was a field of activity in which everyone who took an interest in the matter at all felt himself entitled to know best.

The one thing practically no one then thought was that censorship should be abolished. Tightened up? Yes, perhaps, especially in the interests of children. The opposite was unthinkable, except to a few creative artists and other oddities of whom the country as a whole took little note. In the middle of the decade the Film Society was established, and here it was held to be quite in order for the intelligentzia and the cinéastes to see pretty well what they pleased; but even they themselves were by no means certain that films like *The Battleship Potemkin* and the other Russian masterpieces of this era should be unleashed among the populace at large to preach red revolution to the working man.

The twenties were a curious and baffling period for the working man, in so far as he had the time or the inclination to take notice of what the rest of the country had to say about him. Intellectual snobbery was becoming increasingly fashionable, while social snobbery had not yet gone out. The working man, and even more the working woman, was vulnerable to attack on both counts, so that it was not then considered unmannerly to impugn the taste of whole classes of persons such as nursemaids or housemaids—a custom now as rare and unfashionable as the housemaids and nursemaids themselves.

If Russian films were considered poison to the masses, American films, the overwhelming majority of all films, were hardly less so; because if you set aside a few score names of actors and directors that, in that decade, became household words, it was taken for granted that American films were vapid and negligible rubbish, inducing in an educated person nothing more harmful than an exposition of sleep, but capable of teaching an uneducated person bad morals and worse history and destroying for good any hope he might have had of acquiring the rudiments of artistic discrimination.

The possible remedies were both fairly drastic: substitute British films for the American ones, or discourage and reduce cinema-going as far as possible. And these twin notions underlay a good deal of what the guardians of the people said about the movies in those days.

The general thinking of *The Times*, in November 1923, was that it was doubtful whether Britain could make, or indeed really wanted to make, films in any quantity, but that for the sake of the country's moral well-being she should bestir herself and oust the Americans, perhaps partly by a customs barrier against foreign films, but also by taking up the Englishman's burden and propagating the Empire's moral values, whether she were really inspired to make films or only facing, with the best of motives, a vexatious chore. 'Our Dramatic Critic', in an article on 21 November, expressed the prevailing mood:

> It has been said that art has no frontiers. But film production is at present less an art than an industry, a stupendous commercial enterprise, giving employment to millions of people and appealing to many millions more....
>
> In the film industry, it seems, the Americans have for some time been having it all their own way. This is another of the many onerous legacies of the Great War. When we were busy at war, the Americans, until they also came in, were busy at film-making....
>
> When Mr Ramsay MacDonald said he was 'sick and tired of the foreign films' a great cheer went up. 'Foreign' meant 'American'. He was sick and tired of seeing nothing but pictures of American places, people, manners, customs and romance. 'What nation', he asked, 'was richer in romance than our own? The origin of romantic fiction (a very happy reminder) was here.' It was odd to hear the Labour leader dwelling on romance. I had expected him to dilate on the

economic and industrial side of the matter, but not he; it was the romantic, imaginative, spiritual aspect of the films that interested him.

The movie tycoons of Hollywood, for their part, did not understand what all the fuss was about. Hannen Swaffer, writing in *The People* in January 1925, records that Joseph Schenck, 'the new Film King of America', told him, 'You intelligentsia spend half your time sneering at films and the other half being afraid of them,' adding, 'We don't understand what you mean by all these English ideas and English ideals. We only know that the public want to be amused. We amuse them; you stand outside and sneer.'

But in Britain, all responsible people were agreed: the time had come for the British nation to have its own films.

This was easier said than done, however. It took British production some time to get up steam, and in the meantime American production was in full vigour. In 1924, the lowest ebb of British film-making, De Mille's *The Ten Commandments* came to London. And, say what you like about Cecil B. De Mille, he was bursting with crude vitality, so that everyone said something, the pressure groups and devotees of the 'art of the film' no less than the others: indeed, the cinéastes became so angry that they said most of all. By 1927 he and his publicity men reached the nadir of brash bad taste, and the arbiters of taste nearly had apoplexy when *King of Kings*, which, containing as it did a screen portrayal of Christ, was refused a certificate by the British Board of Film Censors, but was licensed for public exhibition by the London County Council. Among other interesting sidelights on the Gospel story, this film presented Mary Magdalene as the mistress of Judas Iscariot, and, according to the New York advertising campaign, abounded in 'Dramatic Magnificence, Spectacular Splendour, Riotous Joy, Tigerish Rage, Undying Love, Terrifying Tempests, Appalling Earthquakes'.

De Mille, with his expertise in getting sex and violence past the censors in the sheep's clothing of Old and New Testament religion, epitomized all that made Hollywood least pleasing to the traditionally trained and educated British mind; he was so successful that he could not be forgiven.

It would take more than the Cinematograph Films Act, which came on the statute book in 1927, to make ordinary cinema-goers prefer British films to *The Ten Commandments*. But, like them or not, henceforth, if they went to the cinema often enough, they would have to see some now and then, for the Act provided that British cinemas must show some British films. The quota could be varied from time to time as more of the home-made product became available. The exhibitors objected to this provision of the Act, because the majority of their customers wanted what Hollywood had to give. But they welcomed the other change brought about by the Act—a release from the burden of 'block' and 'blind' booking: that is, the acceptance of sometimes as much as a whole year's programme of films not of their choosing in order to get the ones they really wanted.

The Act did not really satisfy the pressure groups, for the cinema, in this year of 1927, had been winning leaden opinions from all sorts of people. A few typical pronouncements give some idea of the prevailing discontents.

On 7 January, the Conference of the National Union of Women Teachers expressed grave concern at the harmful influence on children of many of the films they were shown. The conference wanted local authorities to raise the tone of cinema shows, or else exclude children from all but those specially approved for them by the Local Education Authority.

The schoolmasters were if anything even harsher in their strictures, particularly a Mr Cholmeley of Owen's School, who held that 'if the product is intended to be a magnet to the young and cannot be described as educational, experience shows that it cannot be classified as harmless amusement'.

In that same month of January 1927 a deputation to the President of the British Board of Film Censors complained about many objectionable films and suggested that there should be a Government official with power to burn films to which exception was taken. The General Secretary of the British Empire Union said that 'it was wrong in principle for cinematograph producers to appoint their own censors. It was tantamount to a prisoner providing the fee for the judge.' Mr O'Connor 'kept his cool' and observed that a committee of the League of Nations had declared the British system of film censorship to be the best in the world.

The Times was in its most thunderous mood in a leading article on 19 January about 'Films and False Values'. It considered that

The Restless Twenties

it would take a good deal more than the imposition of a British quota to put matters right:

> The pardonable habit of men and women of taste in England is not to take the general output of the picture theatres too seriously. Hearing, perhaps, that some picture by Mr Chaplin or Mr Fairbanks is good fun or good adventure, they go to enjoy themselves, or, if they are inclined to rather more solemn pleasures, they see the experimental films for which the Film Society commendably ransacks Europe, and are impressed, it may be, by the force and originality of a German essay in the macabre; but they do not go regularly to the cinematograph at the street corner and see what the world sees. If they go at all to such places, it is when they feel lazy and are in a mood to laugh at any absurdity. In some quarters criticism of film is conducted in the same casual spirit. For these reasons the seriousness of the present position is not everywhere understood. We have consistently treated the films, whether in critical articles or in editorial comment, as a potential art and an existing national influence.... Two principal conclusions emerge. First, there is an honourable art of the films, different in its scope and technique from other arts and worthy of independent development. The existing industry has usurped its name and almost stifled its growth.... If original genius arose, it could not obtain 'general release' without conforming to the rules.... A Shakespeare of the films would be told that Ophelia must be rescued from drowning by Laertes' faithful dog; a Tchekov would be informed that all his scenarios lacked 'pep', and that, in any case, he must invent a legacy to save the Cherry Orchard from the folly of its inhabitants. Here lies the root of our second conclusion—that with few exceptions, the films are dangerous and harmful. They are, in the mass, corruption of the popular imagination, particularly the imagination of children; and this not because they are indecent or directly incite to crime, but because they deliberately inculcate false values....
>
> But is all this, it will be said, any more serious than the blatancy of the old music halls? Can we not laugh it away and say it does not matter? The badness of films is serious because, unlike the music halls, they are taken seriously. They have

called themselves 'The University of the Plain Man' and so by thousands they are regarded. People believe what they see on the screen; they go to the 'movies', not only to be amused, but to learn and to 'see the world'. Bad films have, therefore, the effect of bad teachers, and to put no fine point upon it, their general teaching is opposed to both common sense and Christianity. Their weaker-minded devotees become enslaved by a greedy, pseudo-romantic delusion, which is among the psychological causes of our present discontents; the reaction from them is the reaction from deluding drugs. They will, if no constructive attempt is made to raise their standard, profoundly affect the citizens of the future. . . . A social wrong is being continuously done, not in England only, but throughout the Empire. To impose a quota and call it a policy is to allow the wrong to proceed unchecked in order to help a handful of men to make money by it.

We may reflect sadly that, whether or not the paper was right about the gullibility of the hard-headed citizens of Leeds and Bradford, it obviously did not know as much as we today have learned to our cost about the effects of deluding drugs.

Pondering this unhappy subject of bad films for a few weeks, *The Times* resumes in another leader on 22 March:

The modern democratic world contains so many newly enfranchised and very slightly educated minds that it is more important than ever before to prevent their being led astray by ill-chosen ideas of entertainment and interest which only bore and offend those who know more about life. The public diversion would be all the better fun if it did not harp so frequently upon the same strings, for the true values of life can provide quite as much excitement and humour as the essentially dreary false values which are tricked out in gaudy colours.

It is interesting to note that what then constituted knowing about life was not the same as it is today. Now, knowing about life means a close acquaintance with the seamy under-side, about which the average child in the 'threepennies' in the Walworth Road of those days could probably have taught our leader-writer one or two startling things.

However, *The Times* does concede this much about the new Act:

> The provisions against blind booking and block booking have long been needed, and will do something to restore health to the industry. Even the clauses that enforce a quota of British films, though they are at root unsound, may give a section of the trade an encouragement and an appearance of prosperity from which, it is to be hoped, more solid benefits may follow.

After this grudging concession, could peace ensue? No. For there was a more traumatic development in store: the first stammering syllables of the 'talkies'. This gives rise to a good deal of uneasy speculation in the following year. The new departure is not art, of course; but that may not prevent it from having its own peculiar force, and even a legitimate part to play in informing the public: already, Mr Baldwin may be seen and heard haranguing them from the garden of No 10 Downing Street, in preparation for the forthcoming General Election. And about the same time, British Movietone News comes on the scene. But still the backward-looking British think, and hope, that the cinema will not have to devote too much of its energy to mastering this new trick, just when it has begun to come to grips with the silent film.

However, by 1929 there was no getting round the fact that, whether or not the 'talkies' had come to stay, they had certainly established themselves for the time being. In this memorable year, *The Times* put out another Cinema Number, with Articles on 'Film Æsthetic' (some harsh things to say about the talkies), on censorship, on cinemas and cinema organs, and even on those forgotten men the exhibitors—forgotten, that is to say, except when they were alleged to be overcrowding the cinemas, or getting rich quick by portraying vice and crime to an unlettered public, who, it was believed, were as sheep having no shepherd.

The article on 'Film Æsthetic' is peevish:

> . . . Cinematographs, which began as ingenious mechanical toys, developed suddenly into a means of popular entertainment. At one moment they were little more than glorified magic lanterns; the next, they were crude story-tellers of the Wild West; then, as if by some enchantment, they became a

vested international industry. When the artistic critics of the world awoke to the truth that what was potentially a new art had been born among them, they were too late. The films had already entrenched themselves in error; a great barrier of financial success had been erected between them and genuine experimentalists; the history of the growth of every other art had in this instance been reversed; and there seemed to be no way of return to first principles.

The writer points to such films as *Grass*, *Cinderella*, *Warning Shadows*, *The Street* and *Greed* as evidence that the industry had been trying to feel its way back to an aesthetic basis. But:

Now it seems that the movement may have to wait until the talking films have done their worst. If they succeed commercially, the infant art of the screen may as well be abandoned, unless, separating itself from this uproar, it starts life again in independence and poverty; if they fail commercially, then, the industry dying, the art . . . may be born again.

The leading article is equally critical of the talking pictures and concludes: 'The British industry has been wise not to become too deeply committed. Its conservatism may prove to be its golden opportunity to recover lost ground.'

But let us not think about the talkies too much. What do we want with them, when we have the Wurlitzer Unit Orchestra, described in a lively article by Mr Reginald Foort:

Its possibilities are amazing. It can represent in turn a symphony orchestra, a cathedral organ or a jazz band. An almost lifelike reproduction in sound can be produced for any incident occurring on the screen, such as a baby crying, a barrel organ, or a train starting. Sentimental love scenes, dramatic outbursts . . . and the whole gamut of human emotions can be illustrated with equal facility.

As for the exhibitor, he too has his problems. But unlike most of the other contributors, Mr W. R. Fuller, Secretary of the Cinematograph Exhibitors' Association, displays a cautious optimism about the future of the four thousand-odd cinemas in the country. He does admit that the problems of rationalization are bringing about a very swift and radical restructuring of the industry. It is clear that, even now, the day of the independent exhibitor is beginning to decline; and there seems to be a wistful note in Mr Fuller's voice as he tells us that, whereas Provincial Cinematograph Theatres used to be the only large cinema circuit in the country, in less than twelve months the Gaumont Company has changed from 'a respected renting organization' to a vast corporation including about 300 cinemas; and Mr John Maxwell is doing nearly as well. But he adds:

> In conclusion may I say that the exhibitor faces the future with a lively optimism and a consciousness of the useful service he renders in providing the public with the entertainment so essential to its well being? An intense determination to continue to provide the family audience with wholesome and clean entertainment brings him the satisfaction and knowledge that he is, and will continue to be, a useful citizen.

These achievements and aspirations—or at any rate, this way of expressing them—have gone out of fashion today. But Mr Fuller was perfectly sincere and, on the whole, quite right. Of course there were films that were no credit to anyone. Of course there were some exhibitors who were motivated only by insensate greed. And such films, such people, shed their livid light over the industry as a whole. Says *Kine Weekly* bitterly in October 1929, 'Our films are attacked, our studios are scandalized, the entire population of our industry is libelled. We appear to be the most docile people in the world'.

But in that very month Winston Churchill, as guest of honour at M-G-M's studios in Hollywood, was telling the world that 'The motion picture is an essential part of the rapid forward march of civilization, and as such it is standing in opposition to the brutal passions and hatred which even in our time have wrought conflict between nations'.

And on the very day when *The Times* brought out its Special Cinema Number, other London newspapers had not wholly forgotten the cinema. The *Morning Post* was not enamoured of routine movies: it had given generous space to the correct sentiments of Mr Justice Rowlatt when he had confessed, 'I dare not say how little I know about films, as it will attract attention'. (His lordship, during the cross-examination of a witness, revealed amid laughter, 'Oh, how I long for Monday and income tax cases'.) But on this particular day the paper was still riding its favourite hobby-horse, the proposed establishment of a GHQ for British films, preferably under the command of some eminent person with no previous connection with the industry, such as a former viceroy or a retired general. And the *Daily Mirror* took note of the fact that that very evening people had been flocking to the Piccadilly Theatre for the European premier of *Noah's Ark*, described as 'the first super-sound film'. Neither the *Mirror*'s representative nor the rest of the audience took the film too seriously: one woman screamed at the blinding of Japheth, but everybody laughed when Dolores Costello, masquerading as a German girl, broke silence at last with 'a strong transatlantic nasal twang' and was complimented by her screen husband on her perfect English. Yet the writing was on the wall. The majority of cinema-goers were enthralled with the talkies simply because they talked, just as in the early days of cinematograph film they had been enthralled with the moving pictures simply because they moved. Soon, the silent film would have to take a back seat with everybody except devotees of the art of the film. Sound, which had come before vision in Edison's early experiments, was coming back into its own.

And let us go back to the heart of the matter, to the inarticulate nine-tenths of the cinema patrons, to be reminded of what they really wanted and needed in the years between the two world wars. As unemployment, endemic throughout the first half of the century except in time of war, reached its peak from the mid-twenties to the mid-thirties, the people were disinclined to worry about 'false values' or even about a preponderance of indifferent films. What they wanted most of all was the fulfilment of their basic material needs. Man shall not live by bread alone, but it makes a good start; and cheap warmth in a chill northern winter is a useful adjunct. The managers of the cheapest picture-houses of all in the twenties have been accused, in later works of cinema criticism and history, of mean penny-pinching to line their own pockets; it has been said that when the entertainment tax was reduced in 1924 they should have improved their cinemas instead of lowering the price of some seats. This is unrealistic: how much had the very poorest to spare for entertainment of any kind? They had to go to the pictures less often than my friend Bette of Peckham Rye, or patronize a less magnificent picture-house. My friend Bette was, compared with her neighbours, one of the lucky ones: she was now married to Bill Wise, who remained in good work in the building trade throughout the worst of the depression, though he was forced into premature retirement later by ill-health. (He, incidentally, helped to build the magnificent new black Odeon where the old Alhambra had stood.) Sometimes Bette and her mother each had sixpence to spare for a visit to the Tower Cinema on a Friday afternoon, when the last meal before the arrival of a new pay-packet had been safely chosen and paid for. This famous picture palace was a source of satisfaction to everyone, including the young projectionists. They, I have been told, loved their place of work so much that they sometimes left the back door on the latch so that they could slip back after hours to enjoy a noisy game of cards and play the organ. During working hours they refreshed themselves with hot meals prepared by their families and friends and passed up to them from the street in a basket on the end of a rope. At first they had done their own cooking on the premises, but of course it could not be done in 'the box' and there had been complaints about the smell of the food as it was carried through the auditorium. Despite a bonus of sixpence a time for faultless projection, their job was not well paid. But it had its compensations, compared with earning one's living at a factory bench or not getting an opportunity to earn it at all.

As to the patrons, in this as in the other splendid new picture palaces in the less wealthy parts of our towns and cities, they were getting for their money not just a film, but warmth, colour, comfort, opulent-looking surroundings and a royal welcome from the manager, resplendent in white tie and tails. They were somebody; their approval was of supreme importance.

The managers, for their part, being only human, liked the merry ring of the ticket-issuing machine, but they were also proud of their patrons' enthusiasm: it made them feel good to see the long queue curling round the cinema of a Saturday night. The patrons did not mind the queue either. Like the people who, today, flock in their cars to the summer beaches, or even only as far as a traffic block on an arterial road, they liked to be where everyone else was, and do what everyone else was doing.

The best places for friendly individual attention were still the best of the independent cinemas. I have learned from my too modest informant in Dundee a good deal of what personal service entails.

The old ladies came to the performance early, on purpose to have a chat with their friends, and woe betide the new usherette who did not know who their friends were and where, in consequence, they expected to be seated.

Then there was the patron whose left foot had been frost-bitten in the First World War. He always sat in the same seat at the end of the row near the radiator. When prices went up he did not want to change his seat or to pay the extra. Nobody had the heart to shift him, and so for several weeks he stayed where he was at the old price. Then, of his own accord, he relented and paid more. But this was only a temporary financial setback, as on reaching the age of seventy he, like everybody else of that age at this particular cinema, was given a complimentary permanent pass.

Then there were the many patrons who saw better from one side of the auditorium than from the other. No slavish adherence to rules, with the proprietress on the spot to bend them if she liked, so the rule of 'ninepennies this side, shillings straight across', was often broken in their favour.

Soon there was also the problem of hearing. In industrial districts in good times when there was plenty of work to be had, people were usually rather hard of hearing through listening all day to factory noises, so once the talkies came in at the end of the decade the sound had to be adjusted accordingly: 'You could easily tell when it was right,' says my informant, 'by walking round the front of the auditorium and taking a look at their faces.' Easy for some, no doubt, who have learned their trade and really care about their patrons; but how many outsiders would even think of a thing like that?

Later on, as the troubled twenties merged into the hungry thirties, hundreds of the people were relieved of this handicap because they had no work to go to. In Scotland, special afternoon shows for the unemployed began in Glasgow and spread all over the country. Florence Horsburgh, the Member for Dundee, was one of the humane and sensible advocates of such shows at a time when many censorious voices were raised against the unemployed wasting their money in this form of riotous living.

Queueing for Trader Horn *outside the Empire, Leicester Square,* 1931

The interior of the Empire, Leicester Square, 1928–60

Charlie Chaplin draws the crowds at the Glasgow Coliseum, 1931

One soon got to know the patrons (says my informant), especially the older, lonely ones, for they would come to the office on any pretext for the pleasure of pouring their troubles into the manager's friendly ear. Often, they wanted her to telephone the hospitals for them when members of the family were ill or having babies. They always wanted to pay for the call, but they said they did not know how to use the telephone; a good excuse for a friendly get together.

As for the children, they knew they were specially favoured clients at the cinema of which I am speaking. One evening three small children arrived with 1s. 6d. and wanted three tickets. By now the price of admission for them had been raised to 9d., so they were told to run back the few yards to their home and get some more money. Two were back in no time at all to buy their ninepennies. 'Where's your little brother?' asked the cashier. Being young in crime, the eldest of the party said, 'Oh, it's all right, he's sneakin' in.' And so he was, crawling up the steps. I need hardly say that the manager's heart could not withstand such noble simplicity and no one was turned away.

Another night a small boy, seven or eight years old, was found asleep in his seat at 10 p.m. The doorman knew he had come in about 6 o'clock, so he was wakened and sent home. Less than 10 minutes later he returned to say that there was no one in at home, so the staff found him a roomier and more comfortable seat at the back of the stalls and he promptly fell asleep again. With service like this from the management of the local 'family cinema', the neighbourhood hardly needed a children's club.

The patrons of the family houses, on the whole, knew their good fortune, and audiences at this particular cinema were seldom restive and quarrelsome, once they had settled down after the 1914-18 war. Sometimes a few rowdy teenagers got in, but if they continued to be rowdy the competent male staff, standing no nonsense, got them out again—and no money back, which, in those times of scarcity of cash, meant they were not likely to do anything so thriftless and wasteful a second time.

The source of all this fascinating information wishes to remain anonymous because she maintains that she and her father were only upholding the high standards of personal service which were common in the industry, and he would have abhorred the idea of special praise for either of them. I cannot help feeling that if there had been a prize he and she would have been hot contenders.

But the dedicated managers who set out to perform a social service, besides showing films, did feel that they were not alone. The kindness of the management of the Shepherd's Bush Pavilion in the later twenties made such an impression on a lonely woman patron that she left legacies in her will not only to the manager but to his assistant as well. On hearing this the manager remarked, 'We only gave her the usual service . . . she used to tell us her family troubles'.

Meanwhile, what of the 'circuits', which grew and proliferated throughout the twenties, though they were not yet a threat to the success of the independent cinemas? It is outside the scope of this book to give a comprehensive answer to such a sweeping question: I can only spotlight a memorable character here and there—one outstanding tree in the forest of cinemas and cinema-goers that covered the whole of Britain. Let us go back to 1918, to the beginning of the enterprising career of Charles Brown, who started work as an office boy in the employ of the Clavering brothers and worked for them all his professional life, with such success that he became Chairman of the London and Home Counties Branch of the Cinematograph Exhibitors' Association.

Charles Brown, an active and gregarious young man, soon escaped from his office in Soho to see more of the world. At the age of eighteen he was already taking important films to road-shows in live theatres, which was how, in 1918, many of the big films first reached the public. In this way he went to Plymouth, Bristol and other West Country towns, where the patrons queued all day for the evening's cinema show. Next, he became relief manager on the Mile End circuit, which included the Mile End Empire. His duties included running several house magazines, including the *Rivoli News* and the *Mile End Mail*. 'You gave a précis of the main film,' he says, 'and put something in about the variety show—all our cinemas had variety shows as well as films—and an article on any topic of general interest to cinema-goers.' The cinema-goers must have been reasonably pleased, for according to *Kine Weekly* 20,000 copies of the *Rivoli News* were distributed every week. For all this activity he got, at that time, a salary of £3 10s a week. 'The musicians got far more,' he says wistfully, 'sometimes as much as £22 a week. And the orchestra only played for the first feature; after that the pianist took over. They'd go before the end of the feature, too, if their time was up.'

'The Mile End Empire was a roughish sort of place,' says Charles Brown, 'very go-as-you-please. But it was always busy. We had a talent-spotting show there, as well as variety, and that pulled the customers in. Some of the toughs in the audience there'—he remembers with a certain unregenerate relish—'gave trouble to my usherettes, one of whom came to me in tears. "Out," I said to this young fellow, and helped him to go. The only trouble was, some of his friends encouraged him to bring a case against me, and he won. It seems you must not use more force than is necessary, and you must not go on using force in the street: there, it becomes a job for the police.' A gleam comes into his eye: one can well imagine that to the rough Mile End Road of 1918 it had been worth a fine to demonstrate publicly to other potentially ugly customers that order had come to stay.

By 1927 the young Mr Brown was a permanent manager—of the Shakespeare, Lavender Hill, where in the space of a few months he speeded things up so that they were actually able to get in a second performance on Sunday nights. You dared not start the film before 6 p.m.—in the provinces it was usually later, after Evensong—but if you had a concert first, which was quite legal, you could have the audience all in their seats ready for a prompt start, and then you had time for the second house, starting at 8 o'clock.

It was at the Shakespeare that his brother soon pointed out to him that in the gallery only one in nine of the less law-abiding lads was paying for his seat; the paying customer slipped down and let his friends in through a side emergency exit. 'Well, in a case like that,' says Mr Brown, 'you set the Customs and Excise on to prosecute for non-payment of entertainment tax: it's better for public relations than the cinema bringing the case itself. Then I went along to the Brigade of Guards employment bureau and engaged some good bossy types to make sure there was no more of this sort of trouble. As for me, I went home with one of those thick ropes up my sleeve that they use to cordon off the gangways, just till all was forgiven and forgotten.'

It does almost sound as if the cinema manager were the natural enemy of the cinema patron. But he was not: he just had to be a realist and know his people at least as well as the schoolmaster, the welfare officer and the probation officer knew them. He was a good friend to those who had come there to enjoy themselves and not to make trouble, and indeed, he was a good friend to the whole neighbourhood in the hard times which were just coming upon the nation.

By 1928 the Clavering brothers, who already had about twenty cinemas in their circuit, had built a splendid new one at Upton Park. Just in time for the talkies—Upton Park was only the fifth cinema in the country to 'go over to sound'—and just in time, too, for the worst of the depression. Mr Brown, who had already graduated from the Shakespeare to Leyton, was made manager, somewhat to the chagrin of the other applicants, who were all older than he. He advertised for staff, including twenty-eight pretty usherettes, who were all to be 5 ft. 4 in. tall, so that the pretty, mini-skirted uniforms would fit everybody. Unemployment was so bad locally already that there was a queue of 200 applicants. Upton Park Cinema cared about the unemployed. Few other industries—and certainly no other entertainment industry—could afford to care too much. But as sound took over the big cinemas were flourishing. 'The seating capacity of Upton Park,' says Charles Brown, 'was 2,100. One night I managed to accommodate 9,000.'

At Upton Park they gave a practical demonstration of their concern for the unemployed by not dispensing with the services of the orchestra. Variety was a great feature of the programmes at this, as indeed at many of the larger cinemas; so there was still room for the orchestra, even with the coming of sound. But it could quite easily have been paid off, almost certainly with no other job to go to, and local union men took appreciative note of the fact that it was not. Indeed, busmen at the local garage were advised to patronize Upton Park.

In his brief sojourn at Upton Park, Mr Brown learned a good deal about Londoners of the late twenties. He also learned, painfully, some hard facts about London town as it was then. Fog is terrifying enough to travellers on the modern motorways, but since the Clean Air Act of 1956 it has little power to grieve and annoy people who are snugly ensconced within four walls. It was different then. The fog penetrated the cinema; chloride cleared the air, but it made the patrons cough so violently that it was only a desperate expedient for a short time. It ruined a show which Mr Brown put on for exhibitors from all over the country. Another night, without benefit of chloride, the air in the cinema became so black that you could not see Al Jolson's blackened face on the screen; the audience had to be sent home. By 9 p.m. the air outside and inside the cinema was perfectly clear. You could learn a good deal about the management of people in the London of the twenties and thirties, but against the elements you could not win.

At Upton Park during Charles Brown's tenure of office the patrons got the very best of the new talking films, and in addition, Tommy Trinder, Naughton and Gold, an eight-piano show and an early variant of *In Town Tonight* which gave them glimpses of such famous personalities as Gloria, the famous model, and Alcock and Brown. For all this, they paid from sixpence to two shillings. The stubborn, unconquerable 'ordinary people' of London were to show their quality less than ten years later. They would not have been defeated by the mere absence of the big cinemas. But these places of entertainment gave their lives a touch of lustre and gaiety of which they stood in great need.

In 1930 Mr Brown moved on to the Carlton Cinema in Islington. He was still the youngest London manager, but he had learned more than some of his elders about the curious ups and downs of a manager's life. And there was more to come. 'In the early thirties,' he says, 'some of our most constant patrons were the Sabini race gang, who used to come in every Monday afternoon because there was no racing. Of course, when I first came I had no idea of the identity of this gang of roughs who were larking about making trouble in the balcony. "You can't come in here and play up like that," I said, "if you can't behave, you'll have to go." The staff were white with fear, and perhaps I would have been if I had known whom I was taking on. But they were so astonished that they behaved like lambs from that day.'

'Another day,' he says, 'there was a tragic incident. A man was found dead in the stalls. We called the proper authorities and then made sure that the man appeared to be helped out on his feet. One can't have the other patrons upset.'

I asked him if he had found accosting a problem, bearing in mind the constant anxieties of the preceding generation on that score. 'Oh, no,' he said, 'not really. You see, if you have a *wise usherette*, she soon notices if people are changing seats.' An ordinary member of the cinema audience is apt to forget that there is more to being an usherette than wearing a pretty uniform and shining a torch. I find it rather charming to think of wisdom descending like a mantle upon the shoulders of the lucky young lasses who managed to escape from the dole queue into the Carlton Cinema, Essex Road.

Next, the indefatigable Mr Brown was posted to Lancashire. Starting off at Nelson, by the height of the depression he found himself at Rawtenstall. 'The men were nearly all out of work,' he said. 'But somehow, the families still managed to come to the cinema. One reason was the prizes for lucky tickets—tea, sugar, packets of bacon and all kinds of groceries.'

If you add a spice of gambling to glamour, fan-worship, music, the bright lights and the friendly dark—not to mention the more practical advantages of more warmth and comfort than the patron can afford in his own home—you will of course make money. You will deserve to; for you will have become Public Benefactor Number One.

Your attitude to films will not be that of the cinéaste viewing films in a private theatre with a few like-minded people, and he may accuse you of philistinism. For in the last resort there can only be one answer to the question, which comes first, several hundred people or several miles of film? And whoever else is tempted to forget that people come before film-stock, the cinema manager never can, for a good many reasons besides the obvious one that the cinema would have to close down if their money did not keep it open. We cannot leave the twenties without recalling that terrible happening in a Paisley picture house, recorded in *Kine Weekly* on 2 January 1930—how at a special Hogmanay matinée, 69 children were killed and 150 admitted to hospital after a film had begun to smoulder in the rewind room, giving off smoke and fumes. Many children fell on top of one another and were crushed in the resultant panic stampede to escape. The manager was charged with culpable homicide. This is the spectre which, in those days before safety film stock, stood at every manager's elbow. And in a lesser degree, it still does now, for panic, not fire, is the real killer, and the management of people in an emergency, and the care of people all the time, is the true essence of the job. The moral risks run by people in cinemas are still, after all these years, largely a matter for conjecture; their physical safety, health and welfare, on nearly all the days since cinemas began in this country, is a hard fact which we should not ungratefully forget.

4
The Anxious Thirties

This prolific decade saw the arrival of Spencer Tracy, Maurice Chevalier, Leslie Howard, James Cagney, Bela Lugosi, Boris Karloff, John Wayne, Bette Davis, Gracie Fields, Shirley Temple, Katherine Hepburn, Mae West, Donald Duck, Charles Laughton, Laurel and Hardy, George Formby (top of the popularity polls in Britain in 1939), Fred Astaire, Will Hay, James Stewart, Rita Hayworth, Bob Hope, to name but a few. Some films to remember: *All Quiet on the Western Front, City Lights, The Dawn Patrol, Hell's Angels, The Love Parade, Trader Horn, A Nous La Liberté, Dracula, Frankenstein, Mädchen in Uniform, Sally in Our Alley, Sunshine Susie, Jack's the Boy, Born to Love, Dr Jekyll and Mr Hyde, The Front Page, Grand Hotel, The Ghost Train, I am a Fugitive from a Chain-Gang, Scarface, Little Caesar, Thark, 'M', Duck Soup, Forty-Second Street, Little Women, Queen Christina, Private Life of Henry VIII, Sanders of the River, She Done Him Wrong, Sons of the Legion, Bright Eyes, Catherine the*

Great, David Copperfield, I'm No Angel, Man of Aran, The Man Who Knew Too Much, Roberta, The Thin Man, The Informer, The Little Colonel, Lives of a Bengal Lancer, A Midsummer Night's Dream, The Shape of Things to Come, Green Pastures, The Thirty-Nine Steps, Top Hat, Modern Times, Ruggles of Red Gap, Mr Deeds Goes to Town, Night Mail, La Grande Illusion, One Hundred Men and a Girl, Destry Rides Again, The Four Feathers, Le Jour se Lève, Stagecoach, Mr Smith Goes to Washington, The Stars Look Down, The Wizard of Oz and *Wuthering Heights.*

4
The Anxious Thirties

And so we find ourselves in the thirties, that dark decade which began with the worst of the depression and ended in world war. Perhaps it was fortunate that few ordinary people could foresee the future, for there was little they could have done to change it, and the evil of the day was sufficient to bear. However, without the weight of foreknowledge, they did endure their misfortunes stoically enough. And they had their simple pleasures, prominent among which were their weekly or even more frequent visits to the cinema.

The movies were the mixed bag they had always been. There were not enough good films to go round; and in particular there were not enough good British films to fill the varying quota required in pursuance of the Cinematograph Films Act of 1927, so that cheap and silly 'quota quickies' were part of most people's cinema diet if they went at all regularly. But all the same, the thirties were, from the dedicated film-goer's point of view, a period of unparallelled richness and variety. The great Russian school of film-makers had not yet spent its force: *Earth* arrived in 1930. Then arose the famous German school that produced films like *Kameradschaft* and *Mädchen in Uniform*; while some devotees of 'film' transferred their allegiance to France, to *La Femme du Boulanger*, *La Kermesse Héroique*, *La Bête Humaine*, *Le Jour se Lève* and the comedies of Réné Clair. The British school was hardly great in its own right, but it discovered, though it soon relinquished to Hollywood, the director Hitchcock and a whole galaxy of stars; and it purloined from the stage the Aldwych farces, still remembered with affection by all whose cinema-going had then begun. And Hollywood was then at the height of its exuberance and glory: the great gangster films like *Scarface* and *Little Caesar* shot their way through to fame, closely attended a year or two later by the supremacy of the great ladies of the screen in what then passed for sophisticated stories—Greta Garbo, still and always unique, Constance Bennett, Joan Crawford, Norma Shearer, Jean Harlow, Carole Lombard, the inimitable Mae West; later came the infant prodigy Shirley Temple, and later still Deanna Durbin, the schoolgirl's delight. To make the girls swoon there were Gilbert and Powell and Gable and Bogart, Taylor and Cooper and Colman and Tracey and a host of others. Most of them, I must confess, did not make me swoon, though my heart did turn over at the sight of Leslie Howard; but they, and simpler home-grown talents like those of George Formby and Gracie Fields, were greeted by millions of film-fans with transports of delight. Fan-worship endured all through the thirties: as late as 1937 Robert Taylor had to be given police protection when he arrived in England to film *A Yank at Oxford*.

If your particular preference was zany farce, there were the Marx brothers, flourishing right through the decade; if, like millions, you preferred singing and dancing, you could have Jeanette Macdonald, or the Busby Berkeley musicals, or Crosby, or Astaire and Rogers, who were greatly loved by the ordinary cinema-goer, though not so well thought of by the devotees of 'film' who frequented the Everyman Cinema in Hampstead. And, of course, Disney was in a class by himself, 'onelie begetter' of hundreds of characters who found favour alike with the cinéastes and with those who came to the cinema with an uncritical anxiety to be pleased. And for those who wanted something more hair-raising than Mickey Mouse and Donald Duck, or even than *Snow White and the Seven Dwarfs* (which towards the end of this period, got an A certificate from the British Board of Film Censors, though it looks pretty tame to a generation reared on 'Dr Who'), there were Dr Jekyll and Mr Hyde, attended by Dracula and Frankenstein's monster and a supporting rout of werewolves and mummies and monsters of all kinds.

For those with more prosaic tastes, factual and 'documentary' films were on the increase and were being presented with imaginative flair. In Britain, Grierson's documentary films were in the ascendant in the first half of the decade, and Robert Flaherty from the States won acclaim with *Man of Aran*. And the first British all-news cinema, the Avenue in Shaftesbury Avenue, opened in 1930, concurrently with the final acceptance of the talkies as the pattern of the future. It is almost as if the British cinema industry knew in its bones what would shortly be demanded of it, which was nothing less than helping to weld into one classless, devoted, well-informed body of people the whole British nation, at home and on the fighting fronts. A sort of universal camaraderie had been achieved once, fleetingly, in the First World War, through the native cockney genius of Chaplin, who could not rid himself of his roots merely by uprooting. But a more subtle and sophisticated instrument was needed now, the work, not of one man, but of many. We shall see, at the proper time, how far the purpose was achieved. Suffice it to say, now, that when the child cinema-goers of the thirties reached the testing time of their young manhood and womanhood, the worst forebodings of those who had been afraid of the effects of cinematograph films upon the morale of the nation, and in particular upon the young mind, were not fulfilled.

For it goes without saying that the prophets of doom were still with us, fuller of forebodings than ever with the arrival of sound, which, they considered, inhibited the artistic imagination, added point to salacious dialogue and punch to brutality and, perhaps worst of all, reinforced the contagious American-ness of American films. And they found it impossible to keep silence when the cinemas themselves were not only making such a noise but becoming so huge, numerous and conspicuous that they were impossible to ignore.

Cinema building went on frenetically through the thirties, despite repeated warnings by the Cinematograph Exhibitors' Association that it was costly to equip new cinemas for sound, and that there was hardly room for an increase in weekly cinema attendances in a time of unemployment when so many of even the poorest citizens were regular patrons already. Guileless people who knew nothing about the industry were easily persuaded by speculative builders that a cinema was just what they needed to make their fortunes. Had they not seen the queues, the 'House Full' notices, the accounts in the papers of prosecutions when the house had in fact been over-full on a Saturday night? Yes, they had; and what they had failed to notice was that, increasingly, all the good business was falling into the hands of a few vast circuits with a prior claim on the most costly and magnificent films. There was still room for the old-established independent exhibitor who knew his patrons and gave the wonderful individual service which had been a tradition in the best of such houses since the beginning of the cinema industry. But a gate-crashing stranger stood little chance.

Not only were there more cinemas than ever, but as the decade went on they were vaster and more readily identifiable as cinemas. In earlier years a picture palace had looked from the outside like a theatre or even a little like a real Italian Renaissance palace. Distinctive cinema architecture of the kind that we still know today began with the huge Astorias, the Bernsteins' Granadas, the massive Gaumonts and the new Odeons that, in the later half of the decade, were built everywhere in Britain for Oscar Deutsch to the design of a number of the most prominent cinema and theatre architects of that period. An article in *Ideal Kinema and Studio*, a supplement to *Kinematograph Weekly*, on 10 May 1934, explains how even the older houses must now aim to undergo a face-lift, so that there will be no chance of mistaking them for anything other than a cinema:

> Today the kinema architect does not attempt to outdo all the other buildings in the street merely by excess of architectural detail. He is content to make his façade effective by means of distinction. That is to say, he allows it frankly to express his own particular line of business, and rather than cause the kinema to masquerade as something else, he may often emphasize or exaggerate those characteristics which a kinema possesses and other buildings do not.

So there the cinemas were, brazenly flaunting their dominance in the life of the nation, a perpetual source of anxiety to teachers, religious groups, licensing authorities, *The Times* and of course, through all the pressure groups, to the British Board of Film Censors.

Mr T. P. O'Connor died in November 1929. He was sincerely mourned by the trade, and they looked askance at the appointment, only a fortnight later, of the Rt Hon Edward Shortt, PC, KC. There are photos of Mr O'Connor, looking urbane, and of Mr Shortt, looking severe, in November numbers of *Kine Weekly*, which remarks balefully on the new appointment that 'the sentiment of the industry at the moment is hope rather than confidence'.

It is questionable how much difference Mr Shortt's appointment really made to the daily work of the Board, which remained, as it had from the beginning, in the determined hands of Mr Brooke Wilkinson. But the unfortunate Mr Shortt, pitchforked into the tumult of the early talkies and the accompanying spate of gangster films, could do little which was likely to please the guardians. However, he and his team did their best, like King Canute on the beach and probably with rather more effect upon the content of films than Canute had on the waves. In 1930, while Mr Horrabin and Miss Ellen Wilkinson were pestering the Home Secretary for government censorship of films, and the Birmingham Kinema Enquiry Committee was preparing a report which was also highly critical of the Board's system of classification, these much derided men were busy placing forty-five films in the A category, instead of the mere fifteen or sixteen a year which used not to be thought fit to receive a U certificate. Not as many as Birmingham would have liked, but far too many for Manchester, which, running its own censorship committee, was constantly giving U certificates to films which the Board had classified A. The trade did not fail to notice the indulgent attitude of the Manchester Watch Committee: in May 1931, it accused the Board of being too strict. Probably it was not merely worrying about classification but still smarting under Mr Shortt's warning to producers in January of that year:

> Of late it has been noticed with regret that films are being produced in which the development of the theme necessitates a continuous succession of grossly brutal and sordid scenes, accompanied in the case of auditory films with sounds that accentuate the situation and nauseate the listener. No modification, however drastic, can render such films suitable for

public exhibition. In consequence, the Board takes this opportunity of notifying the trade that in future no film will receive the Board's certificate in which the theme, without any redeeming characteristic, depends upon the intense brutality or unrelieved sordidness of the scenes depicted.

There are strangely close resemblances between 1931 and forty years on. The anxiety about brutal films extended to the headmasters, who at their annual conference in the same month called for new regulations to protect children. In his inaugural address Mr L. W. Taylor, headmaster of Darlington Grammar School, might almost be talking about the boy of today. The boy 'is probably much the same as his father at heart, but he is certainly subject to more disturbing influences' because of the cinema (for which, to a great extent, we today must substitute the television screen). Because of these disturbing influences the boy 'has grown up long before his time'. He 'has reached a state of physical and mental development far beyond that of his predecessors' and more varied and enterprising school activities 'are helping to produce a useful citizen'. But on the other hand, modern town life is 'full of baneful influences'. The home control of boys and girls has weakened and there is greater recourse to the streets. The problem is accentuated 'in these days of trade depression when so many boys are leaving school without employment ready to hand'. Thanks to universal education, there is supposed to be an equal chance of employment for everybody; but really the prospects of the least able are being constantly eroded as 'economy, rationalization and machinery' combine to reduce the number of available openings. And in Mr Taylor's opinion the raising of the school leaving age to fifteen is not likely to diminish the difficulties.

The headmasters deplored brutality in films, but they thought that 'vulgarity and sloppy sentimentality', the 'appeal of the pictures to the sexual side of human nature' and 'the drip, drip, drip of the commonplace' were even worse. Mr Edwards of Bradford Grammar School wanted a parliamentary inquiry.

In fact, there nearly always was some sort of inquiry into the subject going on somewhere or other in the country. At this particular moment the Bishop of Kingston, who had been presiding over one of them, was about to report to the Public Morality Council proposing:

That the strongest expression of support be extended to the Home Secretary in proposals to bring the licensing authorities into closer touch with the film censors, and as regards steps to co-ordinate and develop the powers of the local authorities in their control of cinema theatres by the appointment of a standing committee or in any other way deemed expedient or effective.

There were indeed almost as many different opinions on how to control the perils of cinema-going as there were local authorities. In many cities at this time, including Liverpool, children were absolutely excluded from all A films. The Cinematograph Exhibitors were disquieted by erratic regulations of this kind because as the depression deepened they were afraid that people would stop coming to the cinema in large enough numbers to keep the huge industry afloat. It was an anxious time for all the supervisors and guardians; so anxious that one would hardly guess from their utterances that the patrons were enjoying themselves hugely, not without good reason.

In particular, the patrons were not offended by the American accent of the great majority of talking pictures which so much offended their guardians. The guardians took a little time to realize that the English language would never be the same again, but by 1932 many shared the disquiet expressed by Mr E. Davies, a master at Reigate Grammar School, who asked the Association of Assistant Masters 'whether we were going to lower the standard of the English language to the American nasal twang'. If we were not, we 'must either ban talking films or have them made by people who can speak what we call the King's English'.

And on 13 January 1932, a correspondent to *The Times* wrote: 'In view of the alarming effect the American invasion has apparently had on the vocabulary of the people of this country, may I venture to suggest that, having acquired the habit of "Buying British", we now "Speak British"?'

The teenagers (as we did not yet call them) who wanted to be smart took no notice of such remonstrances; indeed, they did not even hear them, for they lived in a completely different world. They went on practising their own variant of the film vamps' and gangsters' variant of the American tongue, and dressing themselves up to look like stars and starlets, but otherwise behaving pretty much as they always had, though admittedly they imbibed a good deal of misinformation from American and other films. Mr Davies complained that 'the American had no historical sense; he did not see the world from the Englishman's point of view. The film provided one of the strongest means for teaching children history and we were allowing it to be debased'.

Whether 'seeing the world from the Englishman's point of view' was really good history either, was not a point about which we then worried very much. But time and again one does have to remember to ask oneself, not merely, as Mr Newbould asked the Public Morality Council in 1917, what people would have been doing instead of going to the pictures, but what they would have been *thinking* instead. And it does seem that, in life as it was lived by the vast majority of city-dwellers in the thirties, the sillier films were substituting 'false values', not for 'true values', but for a waste of boredom and vacuity.

And there were differences of opinion about how much strain could or should be put upon the understanding and sensibility of the average cinema audience. In 1932 there was much disappointment at the failure of a film of Frank Smythe's Mount Kamet expedition to get a showing in the ordinary cinema. But Mr Dixon Scott, an exhibitor of twenty-five years' standing, wrote to *The Times* from Northumberland, that cinemas

> cater for the class of entertainment that the people's average intelligence enables them to appreciate and that is not a day older than 18 years of age. . . . Let me state bluntly that the average cinema audience is no more fit to appreciate the beauty of such a film as Mount Kamet . . . than the members of a football crowd could be to follow the learned and fascinating correspondence in your columns on the pronunciation of Latin. Film 'magnates' must cater for the audiences who are their regular customers, and deplorable though it may sound, these audiences resent films of this calibre being put before them. I have tried repeatedly in my fairly long experience to 'educate' my audiences, but always with disastrous results financially. Besides I now see that I had no right to do it. They expected me to provide entertainment which they could understand and for which they had paid, not to look down on them from a Kamet-like height and try to elevate them.

On the other hand, it is fair to point out that as early as 1911 a handbook published by *Kine Weekly* for the benefit of aspiring cinema-proprietors had warned against hiring 'rubbishy comics' because it was much easier to persuade 'the labouring classes' to patronize good films than to lure the 'carriage trade' in to see trash. The 'man in the street' did not like specialized films outside his range of experience, but he was not slow to recognize sincerity and depth of feeling in matters of universal human concern. His record of recognizing the 'all-time greats' of the motion picture world was not too bad over the years.

It appears that the English language, and the Englishman's sense of history, were not the only things to be ruined by the Americans. By the beginning of 1932 Dr J. W. Ivimey, Director of Music at Marlborough, is complaining of what he calls 'the dithering stop' in cinema organs, and asking if it is not possible to have cinema music without the constant tremolo, which he supposes has been imported from across the Atlantic, and which has now spread to the American singers in the talking pictures. He adds that children who frequent the cinemas try to imitate this style of singing and so come to 'dither' also. He concludes that 'the whole business is pernicious and degrading and he wishes to protest against it'.

Protest was the order of the day in 1932 as it had been in 1931. The British Board of Film Censors, reviewing the previous year in January 1933, looked back with disapproval and forward with apprehension. Films, it said, had become more daring. 'Even when the story itself is not wholly immoral there appears to be a desire to stress the unpleasant aspect which is best described as "sex appeal" with a wealth of detail which is altogether prohibitive for public exhibition. The board has always taken exception to stories in which the main theme is either lust or the development of erotic passions, but the president has come to the definite conclusion that more drastic action will have to be taken with regard to such films in the future,' and 'this opportunity is taken of warning the whole industry.' It added that far more films were rejected in 1931 than in any previous year: the themes complained of included 'collusive divorce', 'offensive political propaganda', 'prolonged and gross brutality and bloodshed' and 'suggestive themes acted throughout by children'.

The Board may have hoped that the advent of more sexy films

would for the moment take the heart out of the campaign against violence. It hoped in vain. There were many to echo the complaint of a Mr Shaw of Wimborne, who said in the correspondence columns of *The Times* on 24 February that the glamorous gangster films were worse than the sex films:

> It has been my misfortune on my last two visits to the cinema to sit through three films emanating from Hollywood in which the hero was a criminal, and which depicted the adventurous life of the American gangster. . . . It seems to me to be probable that the new and youthful type of dangerous criminal mentioned in connection with the Dartmoor revolt is largely the product of such encouragement.

It is interesting to note that Mr Shaw's misfortune did not cause him to leave the cinema, or deter him from coming back for more of the same: it just never occurred to him, or to several million other people in these islands, that there was any question of forgoing their weekly pilgrimage to the pictures.

In fact, of course, members of pressure groups always go in large numbers to the films they know they will most dislike, thereby helping to keep the 'dangerous' vogue alive. The only really effective action is the one which the local authority can take, of banning the picture. And that is only effective if most other local authorities follow suit. Birmingham banned *Scarface*, but that did not prevent *Scarface* from being a fantastic success.

All in all, it is a little difficut to see why John Grierson, in an article in *Kine Weekly* of 12 January 1933, was so sure that 1932 was a landmark in the history of the cinema because 'the governing class has at long last been convinced of the kinema's respectability'. He went on to refer to the Commission on Educational and Cultural Films, and to point out that 'it is even respectable nowadays to adopt the kinema as a profession, as my Oxford and Cambridge mail constantly reminds me. In this respect the Honourables Asquith and Montagu have less need to apologize for professional kinema than the Lord Byron had to apologize for professional poetry.' All of which was true of a small circle of cinema enthusiasts concentrating on a small number of films; but the average patron of the movies, the guardians and *The Times* went their own way just as they had since the cinema's far-off beginnings. In

The Anxious Thirties

October 1933 there was an urgent appeal to the British Board of Film Censors to 'exercise more strongly their powers of censorship in regard to cinema films depicting scenes of brutality and violence . . . and some of the sensational horrific films recently presented', which, according to Miss Eleanor Plummer of the Public Morality Council, attracted just those abnormally hypersensitive and nervously exhausted people who were likely to suffer most. She 'had heard it advanced, as an argument against taking action against such films, that the majority of audiences were quite unmoved by them'. If that were true, which she doubted, 'it would seem to be the most crushing indictment of all'.

The Times, for its part, was back with our old friend falsity. It said in a leader on 20 November 1933 that really the complaints about 'mistakes in detail made through want of capacity' were missing the main point, which was that so many films presented, not merely 'things as they ought not to be', but things as they never could be and as no sane person would wish them to be in any case. The life of so many films was 'a mere distraction, an escape from that which is—not into that which ought to be, but into that which is not'.

In the following month, back came *The Times* to brutality, but this time it was brutality in newsreels, and the Board (which does not now examine newsreels and never has) not only escaped censure but received the rare comfort of a pat on the back. 'That these horrors should be shown as an adjunct to an everyday entertainment and to audiences sure to contain young children is indefensible. . . . The film industry should not delay to seek the protection which the Board affords against the risk of arousing such hostility.'

As far as the ordinary feature film was concerned, *The Times*, in its review of the year 1933, mentioned particularly that 1932's vogue for gangster films began to decline and that in its place 'a movement towards a peculiar kind of Hollywood sophistication reached its climax in November in Miss Mae West's *I'm No Angel*'. It would seem that the Board's campaign initiated almost two years earlier against the 'unpleasant aspect which is best described as "sex appeal"' had not yet had the desired effect. Indeed, the contagion was spreading; for a year later, in a special showing at the Academy Cinema of films made by and for children, and presented by the Children's International Film Association, there was a take-off of Judge Jeffries' Assize in which 'a miniature Miss Mae West strutted up to the prisoner at the bar and demanded why he had not come up to see her'.

It may safely be assumed that Miss Mae West was on the Bishop of Croydon's list marked 'Not Suitable for Sunday'. The Bishop of Croydon had always been a friend of the cinema, in the days when many churchmen were not. After the Sunday Entertainments Act had regularized the opening of cinemas on Sunday at the discretion of the local authority, a referendum was held in Croydon which voted overwhelmingly for Sunday opening. The Bishop supported this move, but stipulated that the films shown should be suitable for the Sabbath, and himself set up a committee to choose 'Sunday films'. So it came to pass that the exhibitors lost a notable ally; for the Bishop's committee came to the conclusion that many films with the U certificate of the British Board of Film Censors were not merely unsuitable for Sunday but ill-suited to the U category on any other day of the week. This conclusion was valuable ammunition for the National Cinema Inquiry Committee which, two years later, was the leader of a deputation to the Prime Minister to ask for an overhaul of the censorship of entertainment films.

On that occasion the Thunderer thundered:

> Whatever the Prime Minister's decision may be, the deputation on the cinema which waited on him yesterday made out a sufficient cause for anxiety. Twenty million people go to the cinema every week; and in these millions the young, the unsophisticated, the slightly educated are so many that they need protection against evils of which they are hardly aware. Supposing that the distinction between innocent and injurious films were, indeed, only a matter of taste, the taste of a vast number of cinema-goers cannot be held to be so trained and formed as to be capable of deciding right. We make no bones about training and correcting the taste of our children; and in a sense a very great many of the cinema-goers are but children. The public taste may be the ultimate standard; but that taste first needs training, and then, as the Archbishop of Canterbury suggested, supporting by a parallel advance in the censorship.

The article went on to plead for a state censorship. But even *The Times* had not the temerity to talk of the local authorities surrendering their powers: it only said that the exercise of these powers should be 'cleared up', 'reformed' and made uniform: 'Seeing that the right use of a power for good and ill even greater than that of broadcasting is indeed a national problem, the deputation did well to state the case for national consideration.'

Nor was the trade itself always completely pleased with the way things were going, On the commercial side it was worried, as always, about the entertainment tax, the quota and local vagaries in regard to Sunday opening. And to these perennial worries were now added two new ones. One was easily put out of sight and out of mind: television, the cuckoo in the nest, had hardly been hatched when it was kicked out of the nest for the duration of the Second World War. The other, less dangerous, but more irritating because more immediate, was the ruling of the Home Office that 16-m.m. films shows, with their 'safety stock', were immune from the special regulations which hampered the exhibition of standard inflammable film. All sorts of unlicensed halls were now in competition with the regular cinemas. The exhibitors thought this most unfair: 'These films *will burn*,' they said indignantly, 'even if they take rather longer about it than celluloid.' The local licensing authorities, when they let themselves dwell on the situation, thought it dangerous for another reason, realizing that the day of slow-burning commercial 35-m.m. film stock could not be far off, and when it came it might blow the top off the precious edifice of restrictions and controls over the content of films which had been built upon the foundation of the fire precautions.

And even the content of films gave the trade some cause for disquiet. In April 1935 an article in *Kine Weekly* complained that, while sex was a healthy ingredient in a full life, 'Sexuality . . . is the guilty element in bringing the Art of the Kinema into the gutter. . . . The distortions of sex-life and love that we get on the screen probably do very little moral harm . . . but [in thick black type] they keep the family away.' Or, as the same paper added a month later, praising the American Production Code, '. . . loose ethics mean bad business'.

But all was not lost. While it is not to be supposed that anything was ever quite plain sailing from the moral point of view for the purveyors of public entertainment, it would seem that, shortly after the middle of the decade, ethics began to improve and business did not do too badly either—that the years from 1936 to the end of the war were as near as contemporary social critics of the cinema ever came to a period of sweetness and light. By 1939 the Public Morality Council felt able to record a great improvement in the standard of films and register its appreciation of many comedies and wholesome stories and of 'the almost complete disappearance of films with distasteful love scenes'. The British Board of Film Censors had allayed much anxiety by assuring the council that films in which characters appeared in the nude had not been granted certificates in the past and were not likely to receive them in the future.

This was indeed a time in which those who really did not want sex or brutality in their own or their children's entertainment were more amply catered for than they had ever been since the first days of one-reel comedies. It saw the rise of the Christian Cinema Council and J. Arthur Rank and the children's cinema clubs; of Shirley Temple and Deanna Durbin and a good deal of miscellaneous escapist entertainment in which Mr Deeds or his equivalent went to town and God was in his heaven and all—except in the newsreels—was right with the world. Even when the world once more exploded, what was wrong with it was nothing to do with the state of British cinematograph films, which, under the sudden weight of a social obligation which made sense to the people as a whole, began to grow up.

I do not mean to imply that Shirley Temple was everybody's favourite little girl, or Deanna Durbin everybody's favourite teenager. Politically radical sociologists thought that Deanna Durbin, in particular, was teaching the young idea the wrong way to shoot; and what Graham Greene said about Shirley Temple's performance in *Wee Willie Winkie* became the subject of a libel action in which the defendants decided to apologize and pay up. But the majority of British movie-goers did not know, and would not have cared, what was being said about their idols in sociological treatises and a short-lived periodical called *Night and Day*. Shirley Temple and Deanna Durbin continued to do pretty well.

As for J. Arthur Rank, it is outside the scope of this book to assess his influence upon the British cinema scene from the middle of the thirties to the end of the Second World War. A man who was firmly determined to run the show as he believed God would wish, inevitably had his detractors at the time and could hardly hope for a sympathetic hearing now. The fact remains that as time went on his ablest rivals were removed from the scene by ill fortune or death or the demands of war service, or by a very understandable feeling that the other side of the Atlantic was healthier than this side in time of war. So but for the dogged and businesslike persistence of the Methodist miller there might well have been no show to run.

As early as August 1937 *The Times* was in mellow mood. In one leader it forgave the American gangster film its immorality because it was very good entertainment and very true to life; in another it praised simplicity and kindness and goodness of heart as exemplified in *Mr Deeds Goes to Town*, in the work of 'the late Miss Marie Dressler' and 'the late Mr Will Rogers', and after them in the phenomenal rise to fame of 'Miss Shirley Temple', who 'owes her wide success to her sunny disposition'.

The writer concludes:

> When Hollywood is not spending money like water on some Herculean task; when it had no axe to grind, no vested interest to favour, no vulgarity to exploit; in brief, when it is being sensible, decent, and honest; that is when its work becomes truly documentary, and it is then that it ceases to libel its countrymen and presents them to the world as they really are.

The British Board of Film Censors basked in the relative peace of not feeling obliged to reject so many pictures: it even got a certain amount of credit for the more uplifting quality of entertainment films. Mr Shortt did not share in the general euphoria, for he died in November 1935. His reign had been a troubled one, and perhaps not entirely congenial to him, for he had confessed at the outset that he 'was not enamoured' of the talkies, though he admitted that he did not know much about them. Later, he had denied that he felt himself under an obligation to improve public morals, adding sadly, 'My job in life is to prevent our morals being made worse than they already are'. His obituary in *Kine Weekly* was not a glowing economium, but it said what any 'film censor' worth his salt would most wish to hear—that he 'had maintained the complete independence and integrity of his office'.

His successor was Lord Tyrrell of Avon, sometime British

Ambassador in Paris, who made a good start by disclosing that he went to the kinema once a week. A deputation from the Public Morality Council waited upon him as early as March of the following year to express their pleasure at his appointment and their confidence that the recent improvement in the standard of entertainment films would be maintained. In June, Lord Tyrrell passed the compliment on to the trade, in addressing the Cinematograph Exhibitors' Association at Eastbourne. He had one reservation, however:

> The first tendency to which I would draw attention is the creeping of politics into films. From my past experience I consider this dangerous.... Nothing would be more calculated to arouse the passions of the British public than the introduction on the screen of subjects dealing with political or religious controversy. I believe you are all alive to this danger. You cannot lose sight of one of the first regulations in your licences, which states that no film must be exhibited which is likely to lead to disorder. So far, we have had no film dealing with current burning political questions, but the thin end of the wedge is being inserted, and it is difficult to foresee to what lengths it may ultimately lead, unless some check is kept on these early developments.
>
> The distinctly political film appears to be receiving the attention of outside producers. Consequently I think it would be as well, in this early stage, to have one definite pronouncement from your organization as to what would be your attitude towards these films, if, and when, they make their appearance.

The idea that 'the passions of the British people will be aroused' in the cinemas by 'subjects dealing with political or religious controversy' dies very hard among their rulers and guardians. It is not dead yet. The British people themselves, however, seem to take such subjects more and more quietly—in the cinema, if nowhere else—as time goes on. But whether they are applying their minds seriously to what is presented to them, or are merely stunned into apathy by the noise and violence of the debate, I would not presume to say.

Lord Tyrrell went on to say that he had been attacked in the Press recently for banning a peace film, though all he had done was to delay giving a certificate because of possible infringement of copyright. *Kine Weekly* for 16 April confirms the passing of such a film, adding that audiences were instructed to write to their MP's demanding peace. On the other hand, in the previous year Birmingham had refused a certificate to a film called *Blow Bugles Blow*, a Socialist Film Council anti-war production directed by the Labour candidate for the Aston division of Birmingham; and towards the end of the year the *Morning Post*, which had been conducting an investigation into the behaviour of audiences during the showing of newsreels, had found a good deal of evidence of 'demonstrations, not confined to the cheaper seats' and believed to emanate from Jewish members of the audience. It appears that 'Mr. Baldwin is invariably cheered and Mussolini invariably hissed, while Ramsay MacDonald is greeted with laughter or "other noises"' (not specified), while 'Hitler, curiously enough, is received in silence. Patrons complain to the manager instead.'

A *Times* leader-writer, in June 1936, expressed the view that, politically speaking, newsreels were the main trouble: they were at present 'as colourless as the BBC', but they could too easily be slanted by changes in the announcer's expression or in his tone of voice. Later, in 1938, speaking at Wigan, Mr Herbert Morrison complained of 'the undoubted unofficial political censorship of newsreels'. Misgivings by two such different personalities as Mr H. Morrison and a *Times* leader-writer lead one to hope that the newsreels were in fact as dispassionate as was possible in those ominous and evil years. But however that may be, any abuse was for once no fault of the British Board of Film Censors, which did not view these films, even as an unofficial adviser. Most people, for a short while, seemed to agree with *The Times* that the Board, under Lord Tyrrell's leadership, was 'doing its important work on the whole very well', apart from a certain tendency to be over-cautious.

Mr Brooke Wilkinson (whom we must never forget, whatever the Press and the pressure groups say about the holder for the time being of the office of President) felt happy enough about the Board's present prestige and future security to transfer it in the autumn of 1936 to a beautiful new home, Carlisle House, Soho, designed by Sir Christopher Wren and haunted still, perhaps, by visitations of the creative imagination more real than most of the celluloid shadows which came and went through its viewing theatre. For it is said to have been that very house on the echoing corner of a quiet street where Lucy Manette in *A Tale of Two Cities* sometimes dreamed that she could hear the future coming.

Meanwhile, it is probable that the great majority of cinema patrons and of the cinema staffs who looked after them day by day neither knew nor cared much about the British Board of Film Censors, the Public Morality Council or *The Times*, and very little more about the acitvities of the local licensing authorities, except where these conflicted in some particularly outrageous way with the child's wish to spend as much of his waking life as possible in the cinema, or the parent's wish to go to the cinema himself without leaving the children alone at home. They were still having the time of their lives, in Oscar Deutsch's gaily-coloured brand-new Odeons and the other super-cinemas up and down the country, in the more modest family halls, in remote village shacks and 'rough industrial halls', as *Kine Weekly*'s film reviewer called them, and last but not least in the children's cinema clubs, if they were young enough.

There had been special Saturday film performances for children for a long time now, but many of them had been pretty ramshackle, rough-and-tumble affairs, more gratifying to the audiences than to those who worried about their physical and moral welfare. The 'tuppenny rush' was sometimes literally a rush, with the children charging into the cinema when the doors opened, after which, at a given moment, a rope was dropped across the auditorium and those in front of the rope, the lucky ones, paid only twopence, while those behind had to fork out fourpence. The really affluent walked in in their own good time and paid sixpence for the luxury of the back row. In another hall the pace was more sedate: the children queued for two hours for the privilege of being the lucky first 200 who filed past a man at a table, paid their twopences and had their cards marked. Fifty-two crosses in a year meant that one qualified for the free Christmas party and cinema show. In grander houses, where there was anxiety about the smart, shining foyer, the children were shepherded in by a side door. What they saw was not sensationally harmful or frightening, but it was sometimes rather sub-standard, probably cheap 'Westerns' that no richer patron any longer wanted to pay for in the ordinary evening show.

But the big circuits (and indeed, a number of good family houses) had begun to cultivate the cinema habit among the very young in a more ambitious way as early as 1928, when the Bernsteins started to experiment with the forerunners of their Granada circuit clubs, the 'Grenadiers'. And in 1934 the popularity of Mickey Mouse provided the inspiration for a great new movement, the Mickey Mouse Clubs, where children got not only feature films, and of course cartoons, but miscellaneous entertainment and moral exhortation of all kinds. There was a Mickey Mouse Club at the Arcade, Darlington, as early as 1933; the Plaza at Crouch End, the Regal at Golders Green and the Lido at Hove followed soon after; by July 1936 there were 76 such clubs and by May 1937 the number had soared to 200. In April 1935 the Camberley Mickey Mouse Club had opened with the reading of a special telegram from the King in response to a loyal greeting from the children; the entertainment went on with community singing of the club song, whose words were composed by the manager, after which the manager was invested by the manager of the prosperous Wimbledon club, an old hand at the game, with the proud title of Chief Mickey Mouse. An explanation of the ideals and aims of the club was followed by a Mickey Mouse cartoon and a Western. Proceedings were graced by the presence, not only of members of the town council, but of officials of the Royal Military College.

And in March 1936 Miss Shirley Temple did the Gaumont-British clubs the honour of consenting to become their President.

There was much in the children's clubs to grieve and annoy the educationists and child psychologists of a later age: they soon began to say that such an important aspect of the child's upbringing should not be left to the untutored caprice of the cinema trade. But there was nothing to mar the unalloyed pleasure and satisfaction of the contemporary cinema-going millions. They were film-fans themselves; they were, in the Jubilee year of 1935 and for long after, intensely royalist and patriotic; they liked their children to be indoctrinated with the ideas that 'clean hands and clean face and neatly brushed hair' and 'giving to charity' and not pushing in the queue were good things. And if we look at the rough, hard, hazardous history of our country in the first half of this century, we shall not find this so difficult to understand. Order, cleanliness and safety, where they existed at all, were new, precious and not to be lightly cast away.

As for publicity and a sense of occasion, it was meat and drink to the grown-ups, no less than to the children. The showmen had done their best throughout the decade to ensure that the cinemas did not hide their light under a bushel. *Kine Weekly* abounds in chronicles of publicity and promotion. One of the most engaging is the visit of the well-known hunter Old Bill to the Trocadero, Liverpool, during the screening of *Strictly Confidential* in 1935, accompanied by his owner in full hunting kit, and by a veterinary surgeon whose business it was to note the horse's reactions. The results of this stunt were gratifying: '. . . two police officers were required to keep the crowd back. Traffic was blocked in the street and the rumour quickly circulated that the horse was Reynoldstown, winner of the Grand National.'

Life at the little village cinemas proceeded in a more sober vein, but it was none the less fascinating. In that same month of April 1935, a 'small exhibitor' tells how, in village entertainment, the clean, cheap little cinema with *good sound* can hold its own in competition with the super-cinemas. The manager, with his little house magazine, acted as local purveyor of news, for there was no local newspaper; he acted as banker to the patrons when the bank was closed; he helped put out fires before the fire-brigade arrived; when the last bus left before the end of the show he took the stranded customers home in his own van. And besides being the manager, he was bill-poster, relief operator and extra attendant.

Jobs in the cinematograph world were often jobs for independent Jacks- and Jills-of-all-trades. And the jobs often ran in families, because if one had been about the cinema as a young child watching one's father, one often did not want to do anything else in later life. It was so with Muriel Bickerton, who at the age of nine was answering the telephone for her father and making a record each evening of the box-office takings at the seventeen cinemas for which he was responsible. Despite a certain resistance to the presence of women in the projection room in times of peace, there has always been room at the *top* of the cinema world for able and determined women, provided they had the help of a father or some other well-disposed person to get them there in the first place, and Muriel spent the whole of her professional life in that world, graduating via the supervision of cinemas to the exacting work of choosing and obtaining children's films for the Rank Organization's Children's Clubs.

I asked her the question I had asked Charles Brown about his experiences some ten years earlier: did she encounter the problem of dealing with women who had come to the cinema to pick up men? 'Well,' she said, 'I did once find an usherette pocketing half-a-crown after showing a woman to a seat, and when I asked her what it was for she said it was a consideration for showing the next unaccompanied man into the next seat. So I rang the police, and they sent along some well-set-up young detectives in plain clothes. That was the end of that.'

Another piece of good advice I obtained from Muriel was 'never turn your back on a drunk woman customer when she is in a temper at being told to leave. I have been hit with a handbag through being caught in that way.'

'The competition from other cinemas was acute,' says Muriel, 'so that you had to get up to all sorts of stunts to promote a film. Once when there was a circus film playing I wanted to hire an elephant, but they wanted £10 a day, which was too much, so I settled for a camel at half the price. I should have taken the elephant. The camel sat down in the middle of Kingston High Street and wouldn't budge for a long time. When he did, he raided a greengrocer's shop and then scared a milkman's horse, so that the horse went dashing away upsetting the milk and causing an uproar throughout Kingston. Writs were served right, left and centre. But it's fun to remember; it was even fun at the time.

'And the patrons were so kind. They hadn't much money, but they would bring me in a small bar of chocolate or a bunch of flowers from their gardens, and when tomatoes were in season one elderly couple used to bring me a bag of tomatoes every week. And the worse times became, the more people loved the cinema. My father always used to say, "In times of depression or crisis, there's one place where people will congregate, and that's the cinema."'

Another 'professional' of the cinema world who caught screen fever young and never recovered is Bert Mayell, now accountant and supervisor of the projection room at the British Board of Film Censors. Before ever he saw a real moving picture, his fate was sealed, for as a tiny boy he was so bemused with the glory of the magic lantern show at the local temperance hall that his one wish was to operate the lantern. Next, the Rechabite hall started showing silent films once a week, safety films on a home projector in the middle of the hall. Bert watched the operator rather than the film, and he and his friends soon decided that they could do this. So they formed a company and showed films once a week at the home of a boy who owned a projector. At a halfpenny for admission they could get eightpence-halfpenny worth of custom at a sitting into the living-room to see the standard 35 m.m. highly inflammable film. Bert thought up the even more dangerous alternative of building a wooden shed in the garden to house the cinema show, but this scheme was not proceded with, as they quarrelled about who was to be boss and the company disbanded.

The problem of getting to the 'real' cinema was financial: Bert and his friend collected manure, picked strawberries, picked blackberries—anything, however dirty or back-breaking, was worth while as a means to an end, the crock of gold at the end of the rainbow, the cinema show. Sometimes father, though he was a disabled war pensioner, helped out with a whole sixpence each for Bert and his two brothers, fivepence to get into the show and a penny to spend. Off they would go to the local family hall. Bert, who took his pleasures very seriously, would often come home in tears, explaining that 'the hero died'. It always made Bert weep when he retold a sad story to his dad, so dad contented himself after a while with just asking if he had enjoyed the show. Any tears shed at the actual performance were shed in secret, and wiped away discreetly when the lights went down for the show to restart. In any case, the very young patrons often did not leave when the show restarted. Sometimes they were too absorbed (for example, when 'Miss Shirley Temple' was the chief attraction) and sometimes too frightened to come out, as Bert himself was when he had persuaded a man in the queue to take him in to see an A film starring Charlie Chan. In vain did the management show slides requesting patrons to leave when they had sat through the programme, for even if they had been disposed to obey orders, most of them were too young to be able to read.

But the mechanics of the thing were still, for Bert, the chief attraction: watching the beam of light from the projector dancing about during an action sequence such as a horse-race was enough to turn attention from the screen itself. And when he had no money to go into the cinema, he and his friends used to stand outside and listen to the projection-room loudspeaker.

A few days before his fourteenth birthday, off went Bert to see the Employment Officer at the local labour exchange. 'I want to be an assistant operator at a cinema,' he said. Alas, he found that he had to start as a rewind boy. Never mind, it was better than nothing. It turned out that there was a vacancy for a rewind boy only six miles from home, and he could borrow his sister's bicycle, so transport was no problem. The manager thought it was, but he yielded to the stubborn determination of this young applicant and took him on at 10s. a week, less 4d. for the unemployment stamp. 'I'd have done it for 5s.,' says Bert.

The Monday after leaving school, at 9.30 sharp, up he went to 'the box', only to find that his morning job was helping the doorman to clean the cinema. Collecting and burning mountains of rubbish from the auditorium took all morning, after which it was back home—six miles—to lunch, and back to the cinema again with his tea in his pocket for the 2 o'clock start of the afternoon show. This was a 'second-run' house, so the programme changed midweek and there was another programme on Sundays—plenty of variety when the newest recruit had time to look at the film. And soon the other rewind boy left and was replaced by Bert's school friend, so he had company on his daily twenty-four miles of cycling.

Actually, there was soon rather more cycling than that, for a new manager arrived at the cinema, who wanted Bert to fetch his hot lunch from his lodgings in the town; so as soon as the boy arrived back from his lunch, off he went again. This went on till one day he dropped a plate of hot stew with a fearful crash when his brakes failed at the traffic lights. The manager, a jolly fellow, saw that he had been asking too much, and Bert was relieved of this particular chore. But running to and fro on his bicycle to collect reels of film from the station was a commonplace of 'Ginger's' day, dodging through the trams in Shirley High Street down to Southampton Town Station. One rush job was the collection of a topical newsreel of the sinking of an American gunboat by the Japanese off the coast of China. The 'topical newsreel' turned out to be a 'Three Stooges' comedy arriving about four hours too late for the children's matinée. It was just another hazard of the job.

All in all, there was not much time for this teenager of the thirties to take the weight off his feet. He did have a tea-break at about 4 o'clock, but at 5 he had to take over from an usherette while she had her tea-break, and at 9 he was away to the off-licence to get the 'chief' his pint of beer.

And yet, Bert was so happy in his work that he never wanted to leave the world of the cinema in which his working life had begun. He did not, in fact, leave it for long, as even when he was old enough to go into the army he took his trade with him and followed it during most of his years of service.

And the hard life of his earliest days did have its moments of glorious discovery. Any treasury notes found during the sweeping-out of the cinema had to be handed in at the box-office, but any coins were treasure trove, to be divided equally between the two boys. At one time the friendly manager found that the doorman had been 'poaching', so he said that anyone who took the coins had to help with the sweeping-out. After that the boys had a free run again. This was particularly useful to Bert, as his sister wanted her bicycle and he had to save up for one of his own.

'I can remember the smell of the cinema now,' he says. 'They all had their own individual smell, not at all unpleasant, compounded of smoke and dust and the disinfectant that was used to sweeten the air. And I remember the chief's tabby-cat, a huge beast that lived in the chief's flat on the premises and had the run of the auditorium: it used to put the wind up many a patron in the dark.

'And I remember, longer ago than that, in the cinema-going days of my childhood, how one day someone dropped a couple of stinkbombs in the queue, and the manager, his waxed moustache bristling with rage, muttered, "If I catch the one that did it—I'll swing for him". And another time some lads kept inflating a balloon and tossing it up into the beam of light from the projector, till the manager deflated them with "Diddums want to play balloons then?" and burst their toy with a lighted cigarette. But there was never any real trouble with the patrons—no rowdyism. And a good doorman could always stop any talking during the show.

'On Sundays the cinema was only allowed to open at 8 p.m.—not a minute earlier, and the film started at about 8.20. One Sunday we were showing *Sweeney Todd, The Demon Barber of Fleet Street*, and we were packed as usual. When the very late end of the show came, the doorman didn't get the glass doors open quickly enough, so he was hurled through them by the surging mass of customers in a hurry to leave. Fortunately the damage was only superficial.

'There were several types of cinemas,' says Bert reminiscently, 'the luxury cinema, all pomp and splendour; the "dump", as some people called the general, run-of-the-mill cinema; the "bug-hutch" and the "flea-pit". All these were terms of endearment, not derision. With hindsight, I can see that the place where I worked

Queueing in the rain for The Great Ziegfeld, 1936

A projectionist at work – Bert Mayell at the Abbey Cinema, Netley, Hants, 1940

The projection-room staff of the Gaumont, Chadwell Heath, 1943

was what other people called a "dump". But to me it was the tops. Our sound and projection were as good as in a "super"—the chief saw to that; and I can look back on the family atmosphere with quiet pleasure. If this was work, it was heaven—a "super" without the trimmings!

'We worked about nine or ten hours a day, six days a week, and my wages worked out at about twopence an hour. In the thirteen months I stayed here, my wage remained the same. It didn't occur to me to ask for an increase—I felt quite well off. But finally promotion called me to another cinema, one step up and an extra 2s. 6d. a week, and no sweeping. But I had overlooked the "perks of the brush", so financially things were the same. However, there was one advantage: the cinema was a mile nearer home, and in rain, snow, fog, and finally the blitz, this had to be considered.

'There was always a full house at "my" cinema, except at matinées, and before 3 p.m. it was sixpence anywhere in the house, with a cup of tea in the interval for good measure!

'Evenings and week-ends there was always a queue outside, and it was a terrific feeling to hear about a thousand people inside laughing at the comedies, or to see them sitting watching a musical or a drama. And one felt very superior, walking into the foyer, past the waiting patrons.'

I have quoted from Bert's reminiscences at some length, because it seems to me that here we get back to the heart of the matter, to what the vast majority of people really cherished most in the picture show, and the unique place which the 'family hall' held in their affections. It is a long, long time from the day in 1920 when Sydney Barnes began his juvenile picture-going in the Scala, New Milton, to the day when Bert Mayell, not yet seventeen, was glad that the journey to work was now five miles instead of six because he had to bicycle through the blitz. But both have a present life and vividness, as one recaptures the emotional warmth of a crowd of people all laughing or crying together over something too guileless to be laughed at or cried over nowadays. And it seems that, fundamentally, and setting aside the top-dressing of super-cinema splendour, the cinema did not change so very much in those twenty eventful years.

5
Chaos comes again

Humphrey Bogart achieved stardom. Gregory Peck made his Hollywood début, Trevor Howard his début in England. Later came Marilyn Monroe and Richard Widmark and, at the turn of the half-century, Marlon Brando and Sydney Poitier.

Some films to remember: *Fantasia, Gaslight, Gone With The Wind, The Grapes of Wrath, Major Barbara, Pinocchio, Pride and Prejudice, Rebecca, The Road to Singapore* (the first of the 'Road' films), *Citizen Kane, High Sierra, Next of Kin, Target for Tonight, Bambi, How Green Was My Valley, In Which We Serve, Mrs Miniver, Obsession, One of Our Aircraft is Missing, This Gun for Hire, Went the Day Well?, Casablanca, Fires Were Started, The Life and Death of Colonel Blimp, Millions Like Us, Song of Bernadette, The Way Ahead, Western Approaches, Henry V, Open City, The Body Snatcher, Brief Encounter, The story of GI Joe, The True Glory, The Way to the Stars, The Best Years of Our Lives, La Belle et La Bête, Great Expectations,*

A Matter of Life and Death, The Overlanders, Paisa, To Live in Peace, Bicycle Thieves, Brighton Rock, It's a Wonderful Life, Odd Man Out, Spring in Park Lane, Louisiana Story, Scott of the Antarctic, Kind Hearts and Coronets, The Third Man and (at the turn of the half-century) *The Blue Lamp.*

5
Chaos comes again

The words 'I think it is peace for our time' struck dread into the hearts of all but the most dedicated of wishful thinkers. The British faced the inescapable facts of the situation and began to prepare for war. By 1939, whoever was still able to put his head in the sand, the cinema managers could not. They still controlled the chief means of informing and exhorting the substantial minority who switched off the news on the radio and bought a daily paper exclusively for the sports pages. *Kine Weekly* knew just what to expect, for twenty years ago is often more vivid than last year to a man past middle age, so that 'last time' was still vivid in many minds. 'The kinema', it said, 'may be called upon to devote itself to a nation-wide series of appeals for recruits, at which a film will be shown and public speakers "connected with the War Office" will address audiences who have paid to be amused. Who would dream of asking similar concessions from the legitimate theatre?'

Indeed, the cinema was called upon for special services even before the war actually began. At Horsham in May there was a demonstration in the cinema forecourt of the treatment of bomb victims; at Kidderminster dummy figures exhibited service uniforms; at Bristol official speakers addressed the audience at each performance; at Andover there were three Territorial parades during the screening of *The Warning*; at the Regal in Manchester members of the services mounted guard during the showing of the same film; at Norwich a short ARP film was shown as a supporting item for *The Dawn Patrol*. *Kine Weekly* carried a leader on 'Frightening the Public':

> ... if we want to see a staged version of a bomb or gas attack upon an innocent group of citizens, we shall have to look in the neighbourhood of some kinema lobby ... we are certainly running rather a severe risk when our entertainment, and ours alone, is the one linked in the public mind with gruesome exhibitions of war horrors.

From all we were soon to learn about the public mind in the Second World War, this sounds as misplaced as the concern of Bottom the Weaver for Hippolyta and her women—'to bring in—God shield us—a lion among ladies is a most dreadful thing'. But it was remembered that there had been sporadic outbreaks of panic in the East End during the first Zeppelin raids, and one could not be too careful. When the blow finally fell, the authorities closed the cinemas altogether, with a proviso that they might be opened later at the discretion of the ARP Department with the consent of the local authorities. If and when they were, it would be necessary for a member of the staff to be stationed in the street so that any air-raid warning could be conveyed to the public.

Within the week, however, responsible opinion had concluded that the danger to morale of doing without the cinemas was worse than the danger of assembling large crowds in one place. On 6 September a letter appeared in *The Times*:

> Sir,
>   I would like to associate myself with Mr Bernard Shaw, who writes protesting against the order to close theatres and picture houses. I do not write this because my son is a film producer, but because of my experience in the years of 1914 to 1918. War is not only dangerous but dull, and it is as important to keep civilians amused as it is to keep them occupied. War work and anxiety are exhausting, and for those who have been through the last war—and hardly yet

recovered from it—I think as much diversion as possible is necessary. I would go farther, and say that music should be played in the parks and in the streets: nor should mourning be worn for those who have died for their King and for their country.

Yours faithfully,
Margot Oxford

The next day, *The Times* reinforced this plea with a leader, on the one condition 'that the audience behaves in a disciplined manner; and no doubt the authorities will satisfy themselves of the degree of popular discipline before giving permisssion for the assembly of bodies of people in conditions where panic would certainly mean disaster...'

On the same day *Kine Weekly* also urged the reopening of the cinemas, pointing out that this move was vitally necessary to prevent the spread of drunkenness.

> If intoxication is becoming a public scandal, if public houses have sold out of beer by 8 p.m., just because people will insist upon being with a crowd of their fellows and there is nowhere else to go, then the time for reopening the kinemas—and the theatres and the music halls—has become an urgent public necessity.

On 9 September the cinemas reopened in all districts except those regarded as most vulnerable to attack from the air, though they closed earlier than they had and some local authorities prohibited the admission of unaccompanied children for the duration of the war. Admissions to ordinary cinemas dropped, partly for these reasons and partly because many people did not like being out in the blackout, with the possibility of being caught, far from home, in an air-raid. But gradually, as the war continued to seem 'phoney', more and more patrons returned. And over the country as a whole going to the pictures became even more popular than before, because whatever the authorities might think of it as a peace-time sport, they had not forgotten that for people in uniform it was the least of a number of evils, a verdict with which the people in uniform cordially agreed. So mobile cinemas were soon provided for the Services, and in addition, except in the most vulnerable districts, they often found that they were better off than the civilians in regard to ordinary cinema-going, for they could enjoy a special show in the local cinema on a Sunday afternoon. The only fly in the ointment was that—predictably—the guardians of public morals were not anxious to extend the privilege to anyone not in uniform; for example, in *Kine Weekly* of 30 November 1939, we read that 'the ban on lady friends of Service men attending kinemas in the Dorset CC area on Sunday afternoons is not to be lifted'. This was unkind, for holding hands in the movie show might not be new, but everyone still liked it, especially those who were far away from anywhere homely and warm and relatively private where they could conduct their courtship in peace. The requirements of courting couples had always been well understood, ever since Mr Newbould and his colleagues had had to give an account of themselves to the inquiry of 1917. Many a prosaic middle-aged head still harbours romantic wartime memories of the two-seaters in the back row (they were called 'Golden Divans' in the Picture House in Campbeltown, nostalgically remembers one of my friends).

When the bombs began to fall, some of the cinemas closed, but most stayed open, supported by surprisingly large numbers of the civilian population. The habit of a lifetime died hard, and some of the reasons why people had come in time of peace were doubly cogent in war. The need for company and warmth were stronger than ever in the face of danger, the blackout and a lonely life, outside working hours, for those who had been left behind when their families went off on active service. As for the actual films, the choice was less wide and many of them were re-issues, but the good new ones were very good indeed and many of them gave expression to that sense of common purpose and dedication which the majority felt but could not put into words. Also, they gave badly needed information: there was no television, and newsreels were more vivid than the most graphic radio bulletin could hope to be, while the informative short films of the Ministry of Information and the semi-documentary longer films of the Crown Film Unit at last gave enough opportunities for all that the British film-maker did best and found most congenial. The cinema-goer was fortunate enough to see *Target for Tonight, In Which We Serve, One of Our Aircraft is Missing, The First of the Few, London Can Take It, Fires Were Started, The Way Ahead, Western Approaches, Went the Day Well?*, and a fair quota of excellent entertainment of a more escapist kind from the world beyond the war—including the epic, unforgettable *Gone with the Wind*, which ran for four unbroken years in the West End of London.

The fine quality of much of their entertainment no doubt helped the citizens to consolidate in the Second War the reputation they had gained in the First, of being 'the most phlegmatic race in Europe except the Dutch'. The patrons needed all the *sang froid* they could muster. Many cinemas were badly damaged. The first big Odeon, the one at Perry Bar, escaped by the skin of its teeth when the demolition workers removed a large unexploded bomb from the foundations. They were rewarded with the freedom of the cinema for ever. Two little boys at Brighton, on being bombed out of one cinema, instead of returning home went on to another. When a cinema in Tooting caught fire, the audience insisted on going on watching *How Green Was My Valley* till they were ordered out by the police. The manager of the Odeon in Leicester Square indignantly denied an accusation that he had the doors closed during alerts and would not let anyone in: he only had the doors closed, he said, when the gunfire became so intense that the audience could not hear the film.

Everyone agreed that cinema staffs were an example to everybody in their courage and devotion to duty. *Kine Weekly* said that if this was taken for granted—and it was—'it is a measure of the confidence with which the patrons look to the kinema for so much more than so many pence worth of entertainment'.

It is perhaps hardly necessary to add that, while all cinema staffs were equal in courage and devotion, some were less equal than others, not through any lack of good will, but simply through lack of capacity, and those were women. Says a news item in *Kine Weekly* on 12 June 1941:

> The girls took their turn as volunteer fire-watchers, two of them in pairs being accepted as equal to one man.... It can be said, right here, that in all matters affecting the actual handling of film, the girls attained a satisfactory degree of skill and, later, when it came to lacing up the machine, they proved very nimble and accurate.
>
> In this, and in all other matters, there were few exceptions to simple imitation. In talking with friends in the Trade about

this aspect, we have, with a smile, likened their learning to 'monkey play'.

And some of the guardians shared this point of view: in Scarborough, for example, in 1941, the police successfully opposed the granting of a cinema licence to a woman. My friend in Dundee, on the other hand, was pursuing her calm, competent way unmolested, not only looking after her own cinema but lending a kindly ear to inexperienced replacement managers who rang her up in the middle of the night for advice and other managers who, on going off on active service, besought her to 'keep an eye on my cinema'. (It was usually not, strictly speaking, their cinema at all, but that was how it seemed to them, the personal aspect being all-important.) In her own cinema, she did even more in wartime than she had done before, choosing 1944 as a good time to start a children's club, with the enthusiastic support of the mothers, who were bitterly disappointed when they were told that the cinema's own trained staff must supervise the Christmas film and party (they found some solace in cleaning the cinema afterwards). The children were equally co-operative: when the sweets and other delights were passed down the rows of seats, nobody kept more than his share.

The guardians had not much leisure, at that time, to see what people were watching on the cinema screen and tell them they mustn't. They had had to go back to the basic requirements of physical safety, with some adjustments to bring them up to date. For example, in certain cities, such as Arbroath (and indeed, Dundee, where my favourite manageress set a good example) it was a condition of the licence that patrons should not be admitted without their gas-masks.

The British Board of Film Censors, however, was still shouldering to the best of its ability the moral responsibilities for which it had come into being. One thing it did to safeguard the tender susceptibilities of British cinema-goers was to suspend for the duration of the war the H certificate which had been introduced in 1933, it being held that 'horrific' films would be unnerving to people under the stress of war. The Board's own staff, for their part, went on coming to their place of work as long as it remained standing. Saturday, 10 May 1941, was the night of the full moon. The bombers came over and inflicted grievous damage on many an

Chaos comes again 139

ancient building, notably the Houses of Parliament and Westminster Abbey, with heavy loss of life. In these circumstances it was hardly worth special mention that Carlisle House, Soho, had been completely destroyed, and that the caretaker, his wife and the local air-raid warden, who had dropped in for a cup of tea, scarcely had time to hear the dreaded onrush of the future when they joined the ghosts of Wren and Dickens on that 'echoing corner' of what had once been a quiet street.

A woman examiner, regarded by the British Board of Film Censors as the equal of one man in the matter of fire-watching (and indeed, in the matter of salary), would have been on duty, but she had changed nights with the caretaker because of illness, so no member of the examining staff lost his life on that occasion, though on another morning one of them did not arrive for work and it was learned that he had been part of the night's harvest of death.

The Association of Cinematograph Technicians would not have wasted many tears over the examiners of the British Board of Film Censors if they had all been on fire-watching duty that night. Only seven months earlier Mr George Elvin, the Association's secretary, had attacked the Board for exercising 'a censorship based on the social, political and moral ideas of our grand-parents'. He advocated the complete abolition of censorship except in time of war, with the proviso that children should always be accompanied by their parents. He added, in effect, that the people had shown that they would swallow politics and propaganda on the screen, and implied that, this being so, they should be made to swallow more and more of these commodities, for 'The power, the creative ability and the box-office pull of the members of the Labour, Trade Union and Co-operative Movements can ensure that the cinema is not a drug but a stimulant upon the life of the people.'

Perhaps what the people had been getting was not true propaganda, but rather the expression of their heartfelt conviction of the rightness of their cause and the skill and valour of their citizen forces at sea, in the air or in the next street. It is very frustrating to be dumb, and all honour to those film-makers who, like Churchill, detecting in the nation a lion's heart, found means to utter the roar. Moulding opinion is another and more dangerous matter, and the urge to have a hand in it had not declined, in fact it was shared by more and more people. *Kine Weekly* looked askance upon this tendency: 'Frequently the earnest solemnity of the propagandist leaves his project like a desert of dry bones.'

Though the upper echelons of the trade did not share the idea that it was a proper function of the unions to manipulate the public mind, they professed to welcome an increase in union membership among the rank and file, pointing out that the Cinematograph Exhibitors' Association was itself a union. They particularly applauded the growth of the National Association of Theatre and Kinematograph Employees. The union men were rather less wholehearted in their expressions of approval of the CEA and of one another: in fact, before, during and just after the war there was a good deal of disharmony between the CEA, the Association of Cinematograph Technicians, the Kinematograph Renters' Society, the Electrical Trades Union and NATKE, and when they finally compounded their differences the next thing that happened was that NATKE'S plasterers went on unofficial strike. The working man, having had a first, tentative sip of freedom, seems to have decided that there could not be too much of a good thing.

So did some of the younger patrons. By 1944 there were complaints that the cinema manager's job was becoming more arduous and anxious because of the growing tendency of some young hooligans to express their personalities by such destructive activities as slashing seats. The war had increased violence in those who were predisposed to violence. It had been even more disrupting in this respect than past wars, because the blackout was on the side of the thieves and villains. Cinema managers and their girl cashiers were particularly vulnerable to attack and the attacks were made with more lethal weapons than had usually been employed in earlier days. We did not hear much about them at the time in the national papers, because worse things were happening on the fighting fronts and newsprint was scarce. They were not spotlighted in the cinema newsreels for obvious reasons, and the television cameras were not yet there. But the trade Press showed a growing disquiet. The big cities in war were breeding-grounds for all kinds of villainy, which might well have been encouraged still further by the wider audience which such actions get today. And unhappily, then as in earlier times, the escalation of violence which began with the outbreak of war did not stop when the shooting stopped. By September 1949 *Kine Weekly* was talking of 'gang war in

Islington, violent assaults on attendants in Scotland, and racial feuds in Liverpool, with the poor manager involved in every case'. For good and ill, great and lasting social changes were beginning. But Britain at war could hardly hear the future coming: its footsteps were lost in the 'monstrous anger of the guns' and in the breath-taking temporary changes that were making or breaking individual lives. Most Britons—nearly all young Britons—had been uprooted and jostled about from pillar to post. The boy next door had taken himself off to a hutted camp or the skies over Germany or the Western Desert or an Atlantic convoy. When he came back—if he came back—he would not be precisely the same person, and neither would the girl he left behind him, if indeed she had been left behind and had not gone off to a hutted camp of her own. And meanwhile, the Yanks had come.

The girl next door might never have left her native land—she probably had not, she probably could not have afforded even the cheapest package holiday abroad, if such had then existed; but she knew about Yanks, for Hollywood had told her. Of course, there were Yanks *and* Yanks. But broadly speaking, the bad Yanks stayed at home and talked out of the side of their mouths and became gangsters, while the good Yanks, the sort who came overseas to fight for freedom, looked like Clark Gable and—as if that were not enough good fortune for any one man—they dwelt in marble halls. Or so Hollywood had led her to believe. Admittedly, not everything that Hollywood had told her about England stood the test of first-hand experience, but surely, when it came to America, Hollywood must know. And the GI's, though they did not look exactly like Clark Gable, were on the whole vigorous, well-set-up young men, not backward in coming forward, and amazingly generous with what money they had, which was a good deal more than the average British service man. Blinded by star-dust, and swept off their feet by the suddenness of the invasion, some thousands of British girls went off to be GI brides and live a life which, for better or for worse, turned out to be nothing like 'the pictures'. Sometimes the outcome was tragedy for both parties to the contract, for the Yanks too had been misled by the movies, which had consistently told them about Britain whatever they wanted to believe. (One film-director, a character in a film, put it very neatly when he told another character who complained that the British army did not behave as he was making them behave,

'*You* know they don't, and *I* know they don't, but the people of Kansas City know they do'.)

This incursion of relatively rich and successful foreigners into the British wartime scene was not quickly or easily forgotten. Perhaps the British cinema-goer of a few years later would not have minded nearly so much that in *Objective Burma* Errol Flynn took that country over without any British help, if Errol Flynn's compatriots had not so often got the girl while the girl's own countrymen were away fighting the forgotten war on the other side of the globe. And perhaps, without all the backlog of ill-feeling, the opinion polls of 1947 would not have indicated that the majority of British cinema-goers thought they could do pretty well without American films—and opinion which, in its turn, may well have influenced the Labour government in its effort to save precious dollars by imposing on those films the massive import duty which, in the seven unhappy months from August 1947 to March 1948, nearly broke the back of the British cinema trade.

The abrupt mutual disillusionment of two nations, in the hysterical atmosphere of a world war, was perhaps the most serious consequence of the remoteness from reality of the Hollywood dream. Perhaps, indeed, it was the only serious consequence, for any large group of people, of that complex of spell-binding and make-believe.

It was no new thing, of course, for individuals of both sexes and of almost any age to be intermittently blinded with star-dust: it had been happening ever since women went into mourning, or even ended their lives, for a Rudolph Valentino they had never had any hope of seeing face to face. It has gone on to the present day, though since television increased the panorama of famous people who could actually be seen, not just read about in the papers, the movie actors and actresses have often had to give way to Beatles and Stones and Georgie Best. But by and large, when it comes to the important things in life, people do know the difference between romantic dreams and human nature's daily food; and as long as they do, there is no harm in romantic dreams, in fact, the lack of them impoverishes our lives. The devotees of 'film' might deplore 'the iniquitous star system', as they were apt to call that alchemy which could make a will-o'-the-wisp out of tinsel and silver paper. But stars could only be made because the public wanted them; and the public wanted them because, somehow, a generous instinct to admire and delight in excellence had not been quenched by the drabness and dangers of their own lives. They knew well enough that physical beauty and luxury are not the highest forms of excellence; but plain living and high thinking can be an infernal bore when one's greatest need is to relax after a hard day's work.

When the bombing stopped—even before the war stopped—the minority who had absented themselves from the cinemas trooped back again. Above all, the children's cinema clubs reopened and grew and multiplied. And now, the majority were under the control, not just of a few potentates of the cinema world, but ultimately of one man, the unrepentant capitalist J. Arthur Rank, who by now had his hands on the reins of both the Gaumont and Odeon circuits. Even if all his lieutenants had been as dedicated, according to their own lights, to the welfare of children as he was himself, this state or affairs would not have been acceptable to the left-of-centre group of new guardians who were now preparing to take over from the right-wing faction who, for many years, had tried to monopolize the guidance and training of 'the people'. Typical of the point of view of the new Establishment was a work called *Sociology of Film*, by J. P. Mayer (Faber & Faber, 1946), which pronounced:

> The State must supervise an industry which is obviously not able to see beyond its commercial horizon . . . we have several hundred thousand British children under an influence which is, to say the least, *very much* below the level of the definite rules and standards of the educational system. What the school builds up during the week *may* be entirely nullified on Saturday morning.
>
> This is naturally not the intention of those who run the children's clubs. They have the best intentions, but the task they undertake is beyond their spiritual, mental and technical equipment. In fact, they do not know what they are doing. The fundamental thesis (and purpose) of this book is not to attack individuals but rather to indicate that the film industry has reached a stage where the old 'showman' type, however well meaning he may be, must enlist the effective, not only the façade, co-operation of the social scientist, the educationalist, the psychologist, and last but not least, of the children themselves. And if it be not willing to enlist the co-operation

voluntarily, the State must enforce it. Here, clearly, is a case where an economic monopoly creates under the cloak of 'free enterprise' mental attitudes which, in their present form, are detrimental to the community as a whole.

He added that the British Board of Film Censors was hampered by ignorance and by a lack of expert knowledge of child psychology.

Meanwhile, in the succession of offices and trade theatres where the British Board of Film Censors had taken refuge since it lost its permanent home, time was marching on. In September 1947, Mr Brooke Wilkinson celebrated his golden wedding. On this occasion the President of the Kinematograph Renters' Society told Sir Sidney Harris, the new President of the Board, that the KRS would like him to know that they had always looked on Brooke Wilkinson as the film censor, throughout his many years of office. It is unlikely that Sir Sidney Harris minded this lack of urbanity. Having just ended a distinguished career in the Civil Service, he expected to be unknown to the country at large, and his attitude to self-advertisement was that of Queen Victoria to expediency: it was a word he never wished to hear again, nor to understand. But all the same, anyone who was actively engaged in providing suitable entertainment films for the world's children had heard of Mr S. W. Harris of the Home Office, who had represented this country on the Child Welfare Committee of the League of Nations, and its successor, the Commission on Social Questions, and had been an adviser on matters relating to children and the cinema for a number of years.

In July 1948, Mr Brooke Wilkinson died, after nearly thirty-four years in office, to be succeeded by Arthur Watkins, an ebullient Welshman whose favourite occupation was writing plays, but who had found his way into the Home Office via fire-fighting in London in the war.

The new team was faced with a demand for a departmental Committee of Inquiry into the effects of cinema-going, and particularly cinema clubs, on children. This the Government felt unable to refuse, but they prudently excluded from the terms of reference the constitution and status of the British Board of Film Censors. They did, however, invite the Committee, under the chairmanship of Professor K. C. Wheare, to consider changes in the procedure for classifying films. This alarmed the trade. 'Let

Children queuing for a Kinema Club Matinée – 9.15 on a Saturday morning in 1948

Queues at Giffnock, when the suburban cinemas re-opened in September, 1939

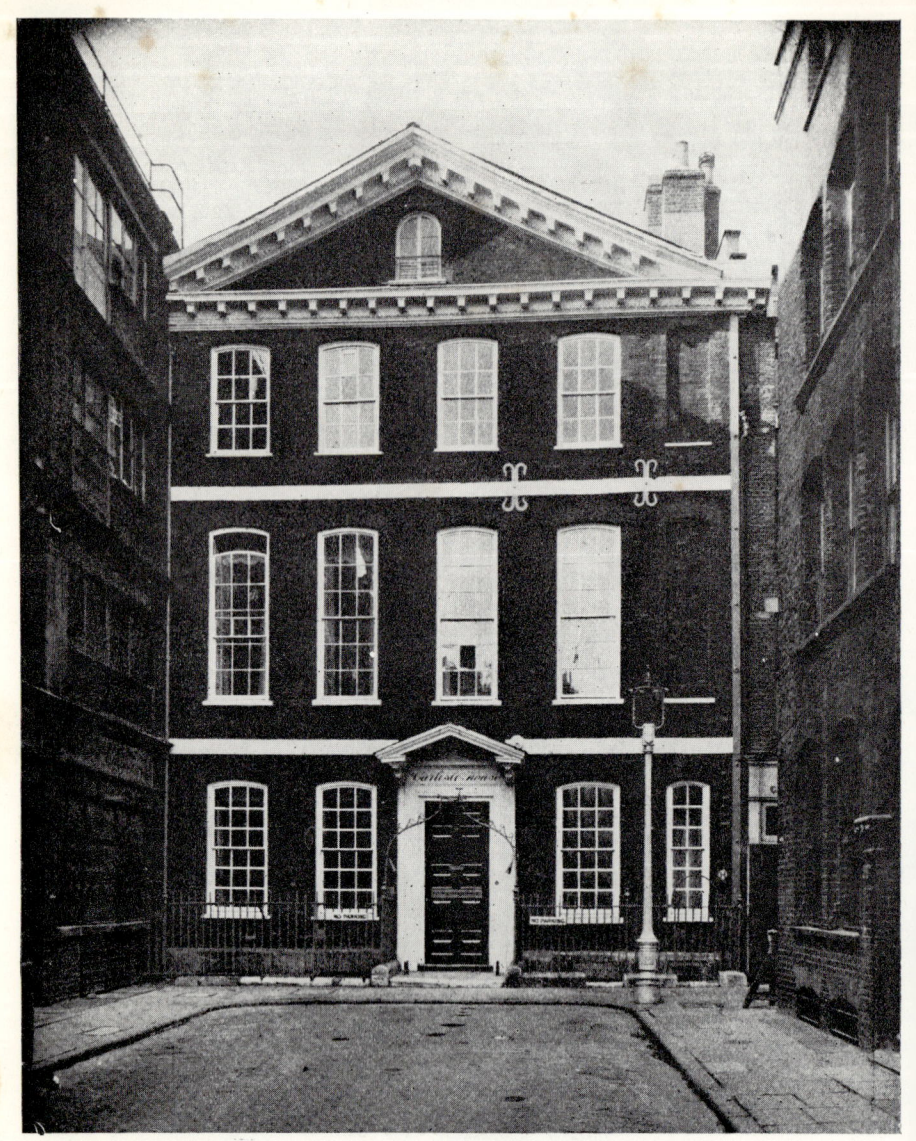

Carlisle House – home of the British Board of Film Censors, 1936–41

Well Alone!' cried *Kine Weekly* on 29 July 1948. '... it is nonsense to suggest drastic revisions when the BBFC record since 1912 suggests that not only the trade, but public opinion as a whole, is satisfied with a censor who leaves the final decision to the people—through every licensing authority in the country.'

The trade had had enough worries without this. Squabbles about the Sunday opening of cinemas were by no means a thing of the past, and campaigning had been particularly bitter when polls were held on the subject in the memorably bitter winter of 1946–7. One envenomed battle had been at Halifax, where snow was piled three feet high in the streets and all helpers had to be supplied with gumboots. A poll of 18,393 decided in favour of Sunday opening by the narrow margin of 1,477 votes. At Bradford there was snow too. At Bournemouth the weather was better but tempers were worse: a representative of Gaumont British was not only shouted down but actually stoned.

Not that the question of Sunday, or any other, opening would be anything but purely academic if the new import tax on films were not instantly withdrawn. And when it was, what about the lengthening shadow of television? About television some of the film men were still whistling to keep their spirits up. But others said (*Kine Weekly*, 25 August 1949):

> Recently a national newspaper conducted its own inquiry into the question of television versus the kinema. The results were distinctly unfavourable so far as the latter was concerned. ... The wiseacres of the industry shake their heads and trot out the old arguments about the herding instinct; the flow of trade from the young courting couples, the youngsters who like to get away from home in the evening. But remember this; the herd instinct can operate just as successfully among neighbours who may gather round one set for their night entertainment—free.

Perhaps it was this growing feeling of insecurity which had made the trade particularly sensitive to unfriendly criticism of their films. Ill will had come to a head in 1947 in a marathon trial of strength, *Turner v. Metro-Goldwyn-Mayer Pictures Ltd*. Mrs Turner, better known as E. Arnot Robertson, had been reviewing films for BBC radio. Her poor opinion of some of M-G-M's films, and in particular of one called *The Green Years*, had provoked the Company to write to the BBC that 'that critic is completely out of touch with the tastes and entertainment requirements of the picture-going millions who are also radio listeners and her criticisms are on the whole unnecessarily harmful to the film industry'. In consequence, they said, they had decided not to invite her to review any more of their films and they wanted the Director of BBC talks to co-operate by restraining her from doing so on BBC broadcasts. She sued them for libel, and won her case in the lower court, but the decision was reversed on appeal. It could not have been a more close-run thing, for at the trial Mr Justice Hilbery did not uphold all the jury's findings in favour of the plaintiff, while on appeal the opinion of Lord Cohen was that there should be a retrial.

The sort of thing that M-G-M had said about E. Arnot Robertson was not new, though most people had been prudent enough to confine themselves to generalizations, as when *Kine Weekly*, in October 1929, pronounced:

> ... the average lay Press critic is amazingly out of touch with the public idea of entertainment.
> However well intentioned he may be, it is outside his idea to put himself in the place of a man who has to sell amusement to a clientele which might regard 1s. 2d. as its average. ...
> The natural perceptions of these critics lack intimate association with the class for which our exhibitors cater.

And eleven years later, on 18 September 1940, there had been a distinctly sour note in a pleasantry by *Kine Weekly*'s licensed jester 'Screencomber':

> Last week when a time bomb dropped near the New Gallery a Press show was scheduled for that day and with the bomb liable to go off at any moment, what would you suppose that Press agent did? You're wrong. With all the London critics here at his mercy, he cancelled the show.

It would seem that, in this matter of criticism, film people in Britain did not know when they were well off: they 'should study the American film magazines and be thankful', as the *Daily Mail* had remarked on 10 November 1928:

This is how one Hollywood critic reviews *Guardians of the Wild*: 'Rex, the "Wonder Horse", is the star; but you see little of him. He's buried under a pile of screaming heroine, half-witted hero, enraged father and leering villain. Too bad a horse can't choose his own stories.'

Port of Dreams is dismissed with 'Nice, if you can stay awake'.

Naturally the early talking films in particular are fair game. 'The best you can say of it is that it talks', says a critic of *Madelon*. 'It also sings and makes whoopee with sound. It's Universal's idea of a full-length talkie. Their first-born, featuring Walter Pidgeon, song and dice. The story is terrible, the acting worse. Germany never had a chance with the doughboys singing as they do in this.'

It seems probable that the more exacting critics hurt the film men's feelings more than they hurt their pockets. Admittedly, readers of papers like the *Observer*, the *Sunday Times* and the serious weeklies were sometimes deterred from seeing a particular film because their favourite reviewer said that it was rubbish. But often readers of film reviews by, for example, James Agate, Graham Greene, C. A. Lejeune and, in the forties, Dilys Powell, had not intended to go to the pictures anyway, but only to enjoy good writing by people whose opinions they usually shared: what reader of the *Spectator* on 11 October 1935 would have left unread, or having read could ever forget, Graham Greene on Garbo in *Anna Karenina* and McLaglen in *The Informer*, a splendidly evocative essay, a work of art in its own right? And in any case the readers of such papers as these were only a small ripple in the tidal wave of the cinema-goers of those years: if they had all stayed away on the advice of the critics their absence would hardly have been noticed.

And when the critics went further than saying that a film was rubbish—when, for example, Dilys Powell in the *Sunday Times*, in April 1948, addressed an open letter to the Censor suggesting a new certificate, 'D for Disgusting', to cover such films as *No Orchids for Miss Blandish*—well, I myself, not yet being professionally involved, availed myself of the privilege of the private citizen and stayed away; but I think that most of her faithful followers were consumed with an avid curiosity which had to be satisfied.

As for the popular daily and Sunday newspapers, for them film reviewing had grown up in the rather slapdash and desultory way described by an anonymous 'Veteran Viewer' in *Kine Weekly* on 6 June 1935. He recounts that when he was engaged as a film critic in 1912 his first assignment was to review a film called *Wild Waves* which he had never seen. It was not, he said, till W. G. Faulkner (who, like our anonymous veteran, became a film viewer in 1912) started a pioneer 'Film Page' in the London *Evening News* that the lay Press troubled to take movies seriously enough to criticize them; and Fleet Street as a whole thought film criticism an office boy's job till the super cinemas arrived on the scene. About 1921 he was told by the editor of a leading Sunday newspaper that the film page was run for East End readers, that the only film news worth attention outside the East End was news of Mary Pickford and Charlie Chaplin.

Before the Second World War the dedicated movie-goers did not really need film reviews, except as a source of information about the story and stars, and they could get that from the local paper when the picture came their way. They would see a particular film because they always went to the local picture palace on Wednesdays and Saturdays, or because they made a point of never missing certain stars, or because a good long queue showed that their neighbours and friends, who shared their tastes, expected to like the picture.

Nevertheless, the popular national newspapers were good friends to the cinema trade. They publicized the colourful lives and loves of Hollywood; they ran popularity polls on British or international stars, like those undertaken by the *Daily Mail* in 1924 and the *Daily Mirror* in 1927; sometimes too they luxuriated in righteous indignation at some too explicit piece of sex or violence, illustrated by eye-catching 'stills' of the offending scenes, or announced, as the *Sunday Express* announced in 1930, 'the trouble with the movies is that they are veering to leering', thereby probably attracting quite as many customers as they repelled. One way and another, they made assurance double sure that when the stars came to London they would be in danger of being trampled to death as they forced their way into their hotels through the press of stampeding fans.

The People knew what the people wanted. When, in 1925, W. G. Faulkner, who had left the *Evening News* four years earlier, vanished from *The People*'s pages too, it began to turn its attention more and more from sober views to exciting news. W. G. Faulkner had been a good critic. He was not highbrow enough for the highbrows: he condemned *Greed* because its unrelieved sordidness was not entertaining. But he was a very competent judge, not only of popular films, but of current trends in taste and entertainment. However, he could not hold a candle to the stars. And that year Tom Mix was expected in London, accompanied by his wonderful pony Tony and his baby daughter Tomasina: the horse was to be stabled in Fox's offices, the humans in the Savoy Hotel. Later, Tom really arrived (photo). 'Gee,' says Tom (in a headline) 'This is The Life'; but it is hardly necessary to add that *The People*'s man thinks that Tom would be more at home on the wide open plains of Texas. A few weeks later Tom has gone home, but Betty Blythe has been kidnapped by brigands: 'Allah will exact revenge' said a threatening letter, explaining that her performance in *The Queen of Sheba* had offended a desert tribe who considered that monarch to be divine.

In 1931 Charlie Chaplin is coming to London, so we have a series of articles on 'The Real Charlie Chaplin', followed, when he does actually arrive, by presumably an even more real Charlie Chaplin, the fruits of a seven-hour exclusive interview with the great man.

And the *Sunday Express*, in 1930, began 'The Romantic Life of Carl Brisson' with an episode headed 'The Girl Who Became Greta Garbo'. Other headlines in that paper in 1934, are 'The Real Tragedy of Doug and Mary', 'Why Garbo Wanted to Be a Falling Star', 'The Ordeal of Marlene Dietrich's Baby Girl', 'When Charlie Chaplin Was Abducted' and 'Clara Bow's Fight'.

And when, in 1937, Robert Taylor was about to come to London, he did not really need any boosting, but it did no harm that the *Evening News* heralded his advent with a series of articles spotlighting the fact that in the United States they called him 'the new Valentino'.

Nor must we forget the numerous popular film magazines, which ranged from competent journalism to weekly helpings of trivial gossip. These had a huge circulation, particularly among teenagers, and they helped the movies to make their undoubted mark on the surface of contemporary life, on transient manners and fashions. Looking back, it is difficult to believe that such light-weight stuff had any deep or lasting influence, but at the time opponents of the cinema feared that it might. Dr Doris Odlum told the Christian Cinema Council in October 1938 that much damage was done to the adolescent, not so much by the films as by publications of this sort, which abounded in 'glamorous, unhealthy and untrue' details of life in Hollywood and caused many girls to spend money on dressing up like film stars. There was danger, she said, that girls brought up in drab surroundings would get it into their heads that all that mattered was glamour.

All in all, it was not the popular Press, or the relatively highbrow Press, which convinced the public that from time to time they were not getting what they wanted but what was shovelled up to them. It was not even Judges of the High Court, though Mr Justice Hilbery coined the phrase. Not until they had more money in their pockets, and soon more choice of entertainment, could the cinema-going millions afford to recognize that they would not necessarily enjoy this week's film at their local, and that they were not really predestined to occupy their usual seats, they could always stay away.

They had not yet begun to contemplate this drastic action when the Wheare Committee concluded its investigations and, in 1950, published its report. It recommended that the classification of films should be divorced from censorship and given to some other, specialist body. This recommendation was not adopted, and indeed it would have been difficult to implement, because distributors were, and are, on the whole very ready to make cuts in their films if that is the only way to ensure a wider audience for them, so that classifying and recommending cuts cannot well be separated.

The Report is a painstaking piece of work and the researches on which it is founded were much more thorough and scientific than those of the Public Morality Council in 1917. But, being couched in the terms proper to a government-sponsored document, it lacks colour, and the quirks and oddities of individual human beings have been ironed out of it. It can be read for information but hardly for enjoyment.

During this time the new men at the British Board of Film Censors had been applying themselves to setting their house in order. Mr Elvin had been less than fair, in 1944, in accusing the Board of perpetuating the ideas of two generations earlier, except in so far as this was true of the country as a whole. The clock had not stopped: the people of this country had been enjoying themselves well enough and had had no sense of deprivation because a few films and a crop of words and incidents had been withheld from them. Indeed, when the Board had come under fire it was often for being too permissive: witness in particular the storm of indignation which greeted the passing in 1948 of *No Orchids for Miss Blandish*. This was an extremely tame film by today's standards, but it attracted huge queues of sensation-seekers to the Regent Street Plaza at the time and caused Mr Tom Driberg, MP, to ask the Prime Minister either to abolish censorship altogether or to replace the BBFC by a State panel of educated persons. But the clock was in general rather slow, which was perhaps inevitable when the only continuing influence during the previous quarter of a century had been that of one man. Sir Sidney Harris and Arthur Watkins began to put the clock forward, not suddenly, but gradually, to tell a time which was fairly well in accord with the people's estimate of what the time ought to be. It was mainly through their efforts that the scope of cinema entertainment was enlarged by the introduction at the beginning of 1951 of the new X certificate, replacing the old H and making possible the exhibition of a whole range of adult films which so far had not been acceptable because of the manifest objection to showing them to children. This was a necessary move. It gave the *coup de grace* to the 'universal family cinema', but that, for a variety of reasons, was doomed in any case. Sir Sidney Harris and Arthur Watkins had that useful characteristic of the ablest British civil servants, the *tact des choses possibles*, without which there is no hope of running society in an orderly way.

Now, of course, time has galloped away with us like a runaway horse, so that the standards of 1950 seem almost as antiquated as those of 1917 to the unsure, perilous, fascinating world of today. We have not exactly come of age, but we have emerged from childhood into gawky adolescence. We combine scepticism and credulity; physical maturity and mental alertness go hand in hand with spiritual childishness. We are by turns compassionate and incredibly callous. We are gradually abandoning class snobbery, only to adopt an increasing snobbery of wealth. We manage to combine the theory of absolute pacifism with a terrifying violence towards people of opposite political views to our own. Almost the only widely held certainty is belief in the absolute right of all men, women and children to be judge in their own quarrel and do exactly as they please. For the years since the war have seen an explosion hardly less disruptive of the old ways of thought than the atomic bomb itself would be of the world's physical fabric, the sudden eruption of freedom into the lives of millions of people all over the world who never had any before. And freedom, so easy to talk about, so glorious to contemplate, is heady and dangerous stuff, apt to make the unaccustomed behave like blind bacchanals and end up facing with thick heads the sober 'morning after' of revolution and a long hard slog to secure the bread-and-butter of basic liberties, let alone the inebriating drink.

Little of this dramatic upheaval was as yet apparent in 1950. In particular, the British cinema-going scene was the same as before, only more so, for this year, in terms of attendances, was the peak of prosperity. But the day of the cinema as a place of universal resort was nearly over. By the early fifties the patrons had struck their tents and were on the march again, they were going home. For millions who had never dreamed of such good fortune now had a home to go to, and in it was a television set, and at the door was a car. And as time went on these things supplanted the cinema as current crazes, for crazes they all became. One householder would come home in the evening and remain glued to 'the telly' till time for bed, another would spend the evenings of his working days lying under the family car and the weekends driving the family to the coast; another would devote all his energies to painting and papering and then scraping all the plaster off the walls and starting again, with the sort of loving dedication that one seldom accords to a slum landlord's property or to a tenement shared with several other families.

The cinema was still to be a popular way of spending one's leisure. Some people would go regularly because they were young and wanted the outing, or because they were old and wanted the company, or because they wanted to be shocked or shattered or titillated to an extent which the family screen in the home did not permit. Some—a great many—were probably more dependent than they knew on the infusion into their lives of vivid colour which the television screen could not yet give and the cinema now could. From time to time, as in the old days, everybody would go, or at all events everybody who was allowed in. For in 1950,

Marlon Brando and Sydney Poitier had only just arrived on the scene; the public knew nothing yet of the Sound of Music or of James Bond; the rising generation had not yet gone rocking round the clock and tearing up seats in cinemas in a rush of surplus energy to the head and feet, or whipped themselves into a frenzy of adulation of Beatles or Stones. There was no news yet of the Rebel without a Cause, let alone the Graduate and the Easy Riders who were to awaken the admiration of the rebellious young. Records of one kind or another were to be broken time and again by these new arrivals, by block-busting masterpieces of hate and violence, and by a huge army of naked ladies and gentlemen from all over Europe and the USA, who shall be nameless, for the very good reason that in their class of alleged acting the name does not matter. Whatever else one can say of the cinematograph film and its audiences in the past two decades, one cannot justly complain that they have all been deficient in life.

But the picture palace that was 'everybody's palace', the cinema as the pioneers knew it, had joined the music-hall as part of the rich popular culture of the past. It had given what, in its heyday, no other medium could: escape into a new dimension of light and gaiety and emotion. In a period which knew more than its fair share of hardship and danger and death, it had given now and then that happiness whose pursuit, we are told, is an inalienable human right, but whose capture no politician can guarantee.

In the art, craft, trade and huge commercial empire of the cinema of the first half of the century, and in the reactions of authority towards it, can be seen the very image of Britannia, warts and all. She was by turns prudish, prurient, full of an earnest desire for self-improvement; acquisitive and greedy at times, yet not without a real vein of religious fervour and a non conformist conscience forever at war with some of the things she did; fiercely patriotic, as she had need to be to survive those terrible years. And there, at the heart of all the tumult and heart-searching, were the patrons, the rank and file of the nation who, for once, having paid the piper, were calling the tune. Spellbound, fidgeting, lusting, loving, frozen with pleasurable fright, weeping a little, eating and laughing immoderately, the secret people, secure in the friendly dark, eluded the prying gaze of the sociologists to remain an enigma still.

Bibliography

The Cinema: Its present position and future possibilities. Report of the Cinema Commission of Enquiry instituted by the National Council of Public Morals (Williams & Norgate, 1917).
Comedy Films 1894–1954, John Montgomery (Allen & Unwin, 1967).
The Decline of the Cinema, John Spraos (Allen & Unwin, 1962).
The Film Till Now, Paul Rotha; with an additional section by Richard Griffith (Vision Press, 1963).
Film Censors and the Law, Neville March Hunnings (Allen & Unwin, 1967).
The Filmgoer's Companion, Leslie Halliwell (Paladin, 1972).
The History of the British Film, 1896–1906, Rachael Low and Roger Manvell (Allen & Unwin, 1948).
The History of the British Film, 1906–1914, Rachael Low (Allen & Unwin, 1949).
The History of the British Film, 1914–1918, Rachael Low (Allen & Unwin, 1950).
The History of the British Film, 1918–1929, Rachael Low (Allen & Unwin, 1971).
Kinematograph Weekly, passim. (by courtesy of CinemaTV Today).
Michael Balcon Presents (Hutchinson, 1969).
A Million and One Nights: The History of the Motion Picture, Terry Ramsaye (Simon & Schuster, 1926).
Mr Rank: A Study of J. Arthur Rank and British Films, Alan Wood (Hodder & Stoughton, 1952).
Modern Theatres and Cinemas, P. Morton Shand (Batsford, 1930).
The Movies (Marshall Cavendish Books, 1970).
The Movie Moguls: An Informal History of the Hollywood Tycoons, Philip French (Weidenfeld & Nicolson, 1969).
The Picture Palace and Other Buildings for the Movies, Denis Sharp (Hugh Evelyn, 1969).
Picture Pioneers: The Story of the Northern Cinema, 1896–1971, G. J. Mellor (Frank Graham, Newcastle-upon-Tyne, 1971).
The Pleasure Dome, Graham Greene (Secker & Warburg, 1972).
Report of the Departmental Committee on Children and the Cinema, May 1950, (Cmd. 7945, HMSO).
The Silent Cinema, Liam O'Leary (Studio Vista, 1965).
Sociology of Film, J. P. Mayer (Faber & Faber, 1946).
The Times passim.

Index

Agate, James, 147
Americans in Britain, 141
Association of Cinematograph Technicians, 139, 140
Association of Kinematograph Manufacturers, 28, 31

Baden-Powell, Lord, 53
Barnes, Sydney, 75–6, 129
Beaverbrook, Lord, 67
Bermondsey Bioscope Company, 26
Bernsteins, the, 108, 123
Bickerton, Muriel, 124–5
Birmingham: banning of films, 114, 121; Futurist Cinema, 48, 79, 81; Odeon, 137
Birmingham, Bishop of, 53
Birmingham Kinema Enquiry Committee, 109
Brighton: Regal Cinema, 81; Regent Cinema, 80
British Bioscope Company, 19
British Board of Film Censors, 30–2, 51–2, 87, 88, 109, 118, 125, 138–9, 144, 145, 150–1; examiners, 31, 36, 56, 60; 1st annual report, 39–40; and newsreels, 115, 121; and rejection of films, 110, 113, 115, 119
British Film Institute, 78
British film industry, 78–9, 86, 87, 92. *See also* films, British under 1927 Act
British Movietone News, 91
Brown, Charles, 98–102, 124

Campbeltown: Picture House, 136
Canterbury, Archbishop of, 116
Canterbury Diocesan Conference 1912, 40

Cave, Sir George, 52
censorship, 30–1, 40, 51, 66, 85, 88, 115, 116; local, 109, 111, 114; possible abolition of, 66, 139; state, 29, 51, 66, 109, 117; and Wheare Committee, 150
Chaplin, Charlie: in London, 149; unifying influence of, 34, 51, 107
children: 18, 27, 55, 59–60, 63–4, 67, 74, 76, 77, 97, 138, 143–4; in accidents, 19–20, 102; 'accompanied' problem, 58, 84–5, 139; cinema clubs for, 97, 118, 122–3, 124, 143, 144; effects of films on, 27, 37–8, 40, 88, 107, 112–13, 115–16; and imitation of crime, 28–9, 37, 62, 63–4; in wartime, 46, 52, 135. *See also* classification of films
Children's International Film Association, 115
Christ, screen portrayal of, 30, 87
Christian Cinema Council, 118, 150
church-going and the cinema, 26, 32, 40, 63, 116
Churchill, Sir Winston, 93, 139
cinema buildings, 17, 21, 54, 80–1, 107–8; best shape, 54, 80; cost of, 54, 80; first purpose-built, 16, 21; interior decoration, 22, 79–82; lighting, 25, 52, 56, 66; luxurious, 22, 75, 79–82, 95, 108; use of existing halls, 16, 48, 80; war damage, 137
Cinema Commission of Enquiry 1917, *see* National Council for Public Morals
Cinema Consultative Committee, 75
cinema staff: attendants, 32, 39,

47-8, 52, 55, 73, 138; cashiers, 39, 140; chuckers-out, 76; commissionaires, 47, 76; dress of, 39, 76, 100; managers, proprietors, 20, 24-5, 26, 29, 73-5, 88, 91, 92-3, 95, 98, 99-101, 102, 108, 124, 133, 138, 140; pianists, 25, 35, 76, 77, 98; musicians, 98; projectionists, 22, 47, 68, 95, 124; usherettes, 39, 99, 100, 101, 125; wages, 39, 67-8, 98, 127, 129; in wartime, 47, 55, 67, 68, 137, 140-1

cinemas: accidents at, 19-20, 102; admission charges at, 18, 23, 32-3, 36, 47, 58, 74, 83, 94, 96, 97, 101, 122; all-news, 107; attendances at, 46-7, 54-6, 107, 152; circuits, 54, 93, 98, 100, 108; comforts of, 33, 94, 95, 102, 136; drunkenness at, 24-5, 26, 61, 73, 74, 135; fire regulations at, 20, 24-5, 52, 102, 117; and health, 52, 63, 67, 102; independent, 73-5, 93, 96, 98, 108; licences for, 24, 25, 26, 55, 59, 84, 138, see also local authorities; mobile, for Servicemen, 135-6; moral aspect of, 25, 52-3, 55-6, 60, 63, 66, 102; music in, 33, 35, 61, 76, 81, 98, 100, 102; number of, 54; popular classification of, 128-9; projection rooms in, 21, 22; refreshments in, 22, 32, 36-7, 129; restaurants and cafés in, 22, 36, 54, 79, 80, 81; rowdyism in, 60, 73, 97, 99, 101, 140-1; safety regulations at, 19-22, 24-5, 54, 58, 102, 138; screens at, 76; seating capacity of, 100; varied attractions at, 80; variety shows at, 98, 99, 100, 101; in villages, 53, 124

Cinematograph Act 1909, 22, 24, 54, 58

Cinematograph Exhibitors' Association, 18, 52, 54, 75, 92, 120, 140; and censorship, 30-1, 32, 111; and cost of equipment, 107; London and Home Counties Branch, 27, 55, 69, 98; and Sunday opening, 27

Cinematograph Films Act 1927, 87-8, 91, 105

Clarendon Film Company, 16

classification of films, 109, 144-5, 150; A category, 32, 84, 85, 106, 109; and children, 32, 38, 52, 84, 111, 126, 151; H category, 138, 151; U category, 32, 85, 109, 116; X category, 151

Clean Air Act 1956, 100

clubs, children's, see children's cinema clubs

Cohen, Lord, 146

Commission on Educational and Cultural Films, 114

courting couples in cinemas, 46, 55-6, 63, 65, 69, 136, 145

Crown Film Unit, 136

Croydon, Bishop of, 116

Daily Mail, 41, 146-7, 148
Daily Mirror, 41, 94, 148
Darlington: Arcade Cinema, 123
De Mille, Cecil B., 83, 87
depression, trade, 81, 100, 102, 110, 111, 125
Deutsch, Oscar, 108, 122
Disney, Walt, 106
Driberg, Tom, 151
drink, 18, 45, 48, 152; spending on, 17, 59
Dundee, 24-5, 73-5, 96-7, 138

Edinburgh, first cinema, 22
Edison, Thomas Alva, 13, 14, 35, 94
Educational Cinematograph Association, 40
Edward VII, King, 34
Egremont, Ches.: Royal Picture House, 48
Elvin, George, 139, 150
entertainment tax, 94, 99, 117
Eton, Headmaster of, 66

Index

Evening News, 41, 148, 149
eye-strain, 56

fairground picture booths, 21, 74
falsity in films, 'false values', 89–90, 94, 112, 115
Faulkner, W. G., 148–9
Film Society, the, 85, 89
film stock: inflammable, nitrate, 19, 20, 22, 78, 102, 117, 126; 'safety', 102, 117
film-fans, fan-worship, 102, 106, 123
film-making cost, 15
film stars, 65, 80, 142–3, 148, 150
films: adventure, 78; American, 14, 21, 34–5, 85–6, 87–8, 106, 107, 111–13, 119, 141–2, *and passim*; animal, 15–16; art of, 33, 35, 66, 79, 82, 89, 91–2, 94, 112; 'block' and 'blind' booking of American films, 78, 88, 91; British, 86, 94, 106, 136; cartoons, 106, 123; colour, 34, 152; comic, 39, 113; crime in, 29, 37, 58, 62, 84, 91; criticism, reviews of, 35, 89, 145–8; documentary, 50, 74, 107; educational, 22, 24, 58, 59, 60, 112, 114; European, 14, 89; 'false values' in, 86, 89–90, 94, 112, 115; farces, 106; French, 27, 106; gangster, 28, 29, 62, 106, 109, 111, 114, 115, 119; German, 27–8, 50, 89, 105; horror, 37–8, 107, 115, 138; moral aspects of, 26, 62, 86, 117–19; musicals, 106; nature, 15, 60; newsreels, 115, 118, 121, 127, 136, 140; nudity in, 28, 30, 118; political, 113, 120–1, 139; propaganda in, 41, 48–9, 133–4, 139–40; publicity and promotion of, 81, 87, 123–4, 125, 148–9; quota of British made, 88, 89, 90, 91, 105, 117; religious, 30, 40, 87, 120; Royal Command performances of, 23; Russian, 85, 105; sex, 27, 40, 58, 59, 82, 84, 87, 110, 113, 114, 115, 117–18, 148; silent, 35, 94; sound, 35, 83, 91, 92, 94, 96, 100, 101, 107, 109, 111, 113, 119, 147; spy, 46; 3–D, 56; violence in, 37, 39, 82, 84, 87, 109–10, 113–14, 115, 118, 148; Westerns, 23, 34, 77, 91, 122, 123
First World War, 14, 16, 45–51, 53, 61–2, 86, 107
Flaherty, Robert, 107
Foort, Reginald, 92
Fuller, W. R., 92–3

Gaumont-British group, 54, 145; children's clubs, 123; circuit, 93, 143
Glasgow, 37, 96; Picture House, 80–1
Goodwin, F. R., 27, 55, 69
Greene, Graham, 118, 147
Greene, W. Friese, 14
Grierson, John, 107, 114

Harman, N. B., 54
Harris, Sir Sidney, 144, 151
Harrow, Headmaster of, 66
Henriques, Mrs. Basil, 64–5
Hepworth, Cecil, 15, 16, 66
Hilberry, Mr. Justice, 146, 150
Hitchcock, Alfred, 106
Hollywood, 93, 106; *see also* films, American
Home Office regulations, 22, 24
Horne, the Rev. Thomas, 40
Horrabin, I. M., 109
Horsburgh, Florence, 96
House, Mrs. C. M., 77
housing conditions, 17, 38, 59, 68–9
Hove: Lido cinema, 123
Howard Association, 63
Hunnings, Nevill March, *Film Censors and the Law*, 28

import duty on films, 86, 142, 145
Institute of Journalists, 15
Ireland, 50, 52
Ivimey, Dr. J. W., 113

Jones, Mr Henry, Liverpool, 30

Kearton, brothers, 15
Kinematograph Renters' Society, 140, 144
Kingston-on-Thames, 125; Bishop of, 110

League of Nations committees, 88, 144
Ledger, H. W., 48
Leeson, Cecil, 63
Legge, J., Director of Education, 58–9, 60
Lejeune, C. A., 147
Levy, Sol, 48, 79
Liverpool, 30, 37, 58–9, 111, 141; Hippodrome, 30; Stoll, 80; Trocadero, 124
Liverpool, Roman Catholic Archbishop of, 30, 40
local (licensing) authorities, 26, 27–8, 53, 68–9, 108, 134; censorship power of, 29–30, 31, 111, 114, 117, 145; and children, 29, 38, 84, 88, 135; and safety regulations, 21–2, 24, 55, 117; and Sunday opening, 45, 69, 116
London cinemas, halls, 19, 37, 52; Academy Cinema, 115; Alhambra, 15, 80, 95; Avenue news cinema, 107; Carlton Cinema, Islington, 101–2; Cinema House, 22; Coronet Theatre, Notting Hill, 79; Empire, Leicester Square, 80, 81–2; Everyman, Hampstead, 106; Hippodrome, 20; Imperial Playhouse, Chelsea, 47; Kilburn Grange Picture House, 79; Leyton, cinema at, 100; London Opera House (later Stoll), 78, 80; London Pavilion, 80; Maida Vale Picture House, 79; Marble Arch Pavilion, 78; Mile End Empire, 98–9; New Egyptian Hall, 36; New Galley, 78, 80, 146; Odeon, Leicester Square, 95, 137; Palace, 80; Palladium, Ealing Broadway, 79; Piccadilly Theatre, 94; Plaza, Crouch End, 123; Plaza, Regent Street, 151; Polytechnic, Regent Street, 13; Regal, Golders Green, 123; Regal, Marble Arch, 81; Shakespeare Cinema, Lavender Hill, 99, 100; Shepherd's Bush Pavilion, 81, 98; Stoll Picture Theatre, 80, 81; Terry's 16; Tooting, cinema in, 137; Tower Cinema, Peckham Rye, 95; Upton Park Cinema, 100–1; West End Cinema, 78
London County Council, 21, 22, 24, 26, 29, 30, 55, 59–60, 87
London fog, 100–1
Lumière, A. and L., 13, 14

Macdonald, Ramsay, 86–7, 121
McKenna, Reginald, 29, 31, 52
magazines: American, 35, 146–7; house, 98, 124; popular film, 149–50; trade, 35
Manchester: Regal Cinema, 134; Watch Committee, 109
Maxwell, John, 93
Mayell, Bert, 125–9
Mayer, J. P., *Sociology of Film*, 143
Metro-Goldwyn-Mayer, 81, 93, 145–6
Middlesex County Council, 21, 27, 69
Ministry of Information: cinema vans, 67; films, 136
Morning Post, 93, 121
Morrison, Herbert, 121
Morrow, St. J., 29
Motor Cars, 152
Muirhead, Mr., Liverpool, 30
music-halls, 17, 25, 52, 89; picture shows in, 14, 16, 21, 22

National Association of Theatre and Kinematograph Employees, 140
National Cinema Inquiry Committee, 116

Index

National Council for Public Morals (Public Morality Council), 115, 118, 120; 1917 Commission of Enquiry, 16, 52–67, 69, 112, 136, 150; 1931 inquiry, 110
National Union of Women Teachers, 88
Nelson, Lancs., 102
New Milton: Scale Cinema, 75–7, 129; Waverley Cinema, 76
Newbould, A. E., 18, 54, 55–6, 112, 136

Observer, 147
O'Connor, T. P., 51, 56–7, 88, 109
Odlum, Dr Doris, 150
Oliver, the Rev. H. E., 40, 41
organs, cinema, 91, 95, 113; Jardine pipe organ, 80; Wurlitzer, 92
Oxford and Asquith, Margot Countess of: letter to *The Times*, 134–5

Paisley Picture Theatre, 67
Pathé Frères, 49; News, 76
People, The, 87, 148–9
Plummer, Eleanor, 115
police, 31, 37, 58, 73, 99, 124, 125
poor people, working people: and churchgoing, 26; and the cinema, 14, 17–18, 34, 38–9, 49, 62, 69–70, 107, 113; living conditions, 17, 53, 61, 64; and snobbery, 85
Powell, Dilys, 147
Press shows, 15, 23, 146
Prince, Val, 79
prostitutes, accosting, 18, 27, 65; in cinemas, 25, 26, 47, 52, 101
Provincial Cinematograph Theatres circuit, 54, 93
public houses, 17, 18, 32, 45, 59, 135

queues, queuing, 84, 95, 98, 108, 122, 129, 148

Rank, J. Arthur, 41, 118–19, 143
Rank Organization, 41, 54, 124
Rawnsley, Canon, 37–8
Rawtenstall, 102
Redford, George, 31, 37, 51
Robertson, E. Arnot (Mrs. Turner), 145–6
Rowlatt, Mr. Justice, 94

Salford, cinema in, 49
Schenck, Joseph, 87
schools, film shows in, 16, 21–2
Scotland, 50, 96, 141; A films, 84; Sabbath, 27
Scott, Dixon, 112
Second World War, 35, 82, 117, 133–42
Servicemen, 45–6, 61, 68, 136
Sexton, Mr., 30
Sharp, Dennis, *The Picture Palace and Other Buildings for the Movies*, 82
Shaw, G. Bernard, 134
Shaw, T., 30
shops adapted for film shows, 16, 20
Shortt, Edward, 109–10, 119
Smythe, Frank, 112
snobbery, 56, 85, 151
Socialist Film Council, 121
Southampton, cinemas at, 37, 127
Southsea: Victoria Hall, 19–20
Spectator, The, 147
Star, The, 47
stealing, theft, 18, 29, 37, 38, 39, 62, 63–4, 65
Stopes, Dr. Marie, 53
strikes, 140
Sunday Entertainments Act, 116
Sunday Express, 148, 149
Sunday opening and shows, 26–7, 39, 69, 116, 117; and charity, 26; local polls, 145; opening time, 99, 128; and Servicemen, 45, 136; suitable films, 39, 116
Sunday Times, 147
Swaffer, Hannen, 87

teachers, 84, 88, 108
television, 56, 117, 142, 145, 152
Temple, Shirley, and children's clubs, 123
tents used for film shows, 16, 20, 73
Theatrical Employees' Association, 67
Thirsk, cinema in, 77
Thompson, James, 30
Times cinema number, 91–2, 93
Times Engineering Supplement, 23–4
trade unions, 139–40
trailers, 16
travelling cinema vans (government), 67
travelling showmen, 16, 40, 48, 53, 67
Turner v. Metro-Golwyn-Mayer Pictures Ltd., 145–6
Tyrrell of Avon, Lord, 119–20, 121

unemployment, 69–70, 94, 100, 107; shows for unemployed, 96
United States of America, 13, 21; *see also* films, American

Urban, Charles, 15, 23

vice, portrayal of, 91
Vickers, Miss, LCC Care Committee, 59–60
village halls used for film shows, 16
Wales: Sabbath, 27
Watford music-hall, picture show at, 14
Watkins, Arthur, 144, 151
Wheare, Professor K. C., 144
Wheare Committee report, 150
Wilcox, Herbert, *Twenty-five Thousand Sunsets*, 76
Wilkinson, Brooke, 28, 31, 51, 109, 121, 144
Wilkinson, Ellen, 109
Women's Temperance Association, 39; Sutton Coldfield, 39
Wormwood Scrubs Prison, 30
Wurlitzer Unit Orchestra, 92

young people, and cinema-going, 62–3, 64–5, 111–12. *See also* courting couples